D1297383

Noel Tyl's *Astrology and Personality* translates systematically for the first time ever, psychological theories of personality into astrological terms and techniques.

It explores the theories of the giants of modern psychology: Kurt Lewin, Carl Jung, Henry Murray, Alfred Adler, Sigmund Freud and others. It correlates their major insights, the unconscious, the hierarchy of needs, inferiority and superiority complexes, among others, with horoscope determinants: the Moon, for example, becomes the mirror of the "reigning need"; Saturn becomes the symbol of the superego; a matrix of the unconscious is formulated among the Houses, Signs, and planets. A major chapter defines psychological terms through astrological notation.

Theory is illuminated through brilliant and provocative analyses of private and public horoscopes, among them Houdini's, Edgar Cayce's, Freud's and Nixon's, the interpretations gaining the dimension of rich psychological analysis. The horoscope becomes a hologram of identity.

This master volume is infused with a vision of the modern astrologer's mission. To be of service, he must be able to integrate the insights of modern psychology. He must appreciate the complexities of his times, so that his interpretations may delineate the "responsibility of individual freedom" within the "grander social whole" and allow for the "management of tensions within change."

Astrology and Personality

Volume V

**The Principles and Practice
of Astrology**

The Llewellyn Syllabus
for home study and college curriculum

The Principles and Practice
of Astrology

Noel Tyl

A complete text for instruction and reference in the practice of
standard astrological methods and the psychological and
philosophical principles for analysis and application. In 12 volumes.

Volume V

Astrology and Personality
Astrological and Psychological Theories

1974
Llewellyn Publications
Saint Paul, Minnesota, 55165, U.S.A.

Copyright © 1974 by Noel Tyl

All rights reserved.
No part of this book, either in part or in whole, may be
reproduced, transmitted or utilized in any form or by any means,
electronic or mechanical, including photocopying, recording, or by
any information storage and retrieval system, without
permission in writing from the publisher, except for brief
quotations embodied in critical articles and reviews.

First Edition 1974

Llewellyn Publications
Post Office Box 3383
Saint Paul, Minnesota 55165

International Standard Book Number: 0-87542-804-5
Library of Congress Catalog Card Number: 73-19913

Printed in the United States of America

To him who knows me not,
whose wisdom illuminates us all,
whose "of" is father to this "and";
To Dane Rudhyar:
this gratitude from one among many.

Contents

To those living in the age of psychological discovery, the words need, tension, anxiety, introversion, extraversion, fulfillment, inferiority feelings, defense mechanisms, the unconscious, and many others are commonplace. Understanding these modern concepts within horoscope analysis is essential for every modern astrologer:

he must know in order to serve.

Introduction

The horoscope is a portrait of the process of becoming, the potentials of development. In dynamic analysis, the astrologer must give his deductions of potential the substance of behavior. The horoscope must be measured as it lives within the lifetime of development.

Astrology ultimately becomes a theory of behavior. In growth, choice, change, expression, and fulfillment, an individual's behavior becomes *personality*. Astrology leads to the understanding of behavior; it is a theory of personality.

In the many theories of personality developed by psychologists, predominance is given to different functional parts of the whole. Yet, all theories agree that no part, no single segment of behavior can be understood in isolation from the rest of the functioning person, the whole. Astrology's law of naturalness (Volume III, chapter 4; Volume IV, chapter 5) recognizes the cohesion of the parts within the whole. As a theory of personality, astrological measurement and evaluation of a structural part must apply throughout the functional whole.

1

This volume relates astrological deduction to prominent psychosocial theories developed by psychologists in the twentieth century. All work together to understand, guide, and appreciate the whole that is personality.

1

Gestalt Field Theory

Kurt Lewin

In Volume IV of this series, *Aspects and Houses in Analysis,* synthesis was achieved predominantly through symbolic relationships throughout the horoscope, the emphasis of hemispheres, patterns, and interwoven aspects. The Gestalt psychologists constructed their field theory in the way an astrologer synthesizes a horoscope: the whole is considered first, the parts are related mathematically, spatially, and the background of the whole gains focus through any part active in time, in a given situation.

The horoscope shows the *field* of personality. In German, the word for astrological House is *Feld,* meaning field. As a personality whole is divided into fields of experience, the horoscope is a *gestalt,* a "structured whole form" of personality. It is a method of representing reality.

The physical field theory in psychology was developed in Germany just prior to World War I by the psychologists Max Wertheimer, Wolfgang Kohler, and Kurt Koffka. The chief tenet of their Gestalt psychology was that "the way in which an object is perceived is determined by the total context or configuration in which the object is embedded."[1] Relationships among components become the determining factors rather than the fixed characteristics of the separate parts.

Kurt Lewin became the leader of Gestalt theory. With the rise of Hitler, Lewin came to the United States and held positions at several univeristies. He died in 1947 at the age of fifty-six, as director of the Research Center for Group Dynamics at the Massachusetts Institute of Technology.

When the Grand Trine was presented in Volume IV, Venn's diagram was used to show the resolution of three different sets of variables focused upon the central personality. Spatial representations can be treated mathematically and often more easily dramatize intellectual constructs than can verbal definitions. —Through a spatial figure, Lewin separates the personality, the individuality, from the environment, the rest of the universe. He uses a circle as the enclosing figure. The boundary of the figure, the circumference of the circle, defines the Self, the personality.

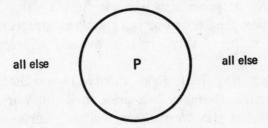

all else   P   all else

1. Calvin S. Hall and Gardner Lindzey, *Theories of Personality* (New York: John Wiley & Sons, Inc., 1957), p. 206.

The interactions of the person with his environment are then represented by another larger figure enclosing the self-core. Lewin called the space between the inner circle and outer ellipse the *psychological environment* (E). Its total area, including the inner circle, represents the *life space,* the personality's overall psychological reality.

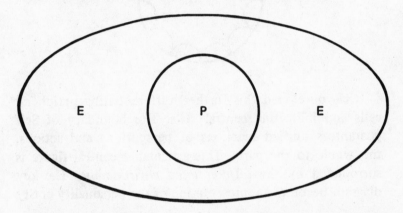

In field theory, behavior is a function of the life space. "The task of dynamic psychology is to derive univocally the behavior of a given individual from the totality of the psychological facts that exist in the life space at a given moment."[2] Outside the life space is a "foreign hull." The ellipse boundary can be penetrated by outside events. The circle boundary can be penetrated by psychological surroundings.

Individuality, *differentiation,* is expressed in field theory by dividing the inner personal circle into cells.

2. Kurt Lewin, *Principles of Topological Psychology* (New York: McGraw, 1936).

Coincidentally (?), Lewin illustrated this diagramatically with twelve cells.

He developed this further, differentiating peripheral cells and indicating central cells. The boundary of Self guarantees unified reactions of perceptions and actions, the whole to the parts. This articulated central figure is surrounded by the *differentiated environment*. The key diagram becomes a representation of the personality entity

defined by cell parts within a life space that is surrounded by a variegated environment.

This is how man finds himself in life: a central core of personality with differentiated cells that give dimensions of intuition, feeling, relating, and thinking (the horoscope's four quadrants); animated in life by the cell parts of mind, emotion, active energy, ambition, vision, etc. (the planets); surrounded by an environmental experience factor (the Houses).

Lewin's figures, by definition, have *boundaries*. Interaction must somehow break down or emphasize these boundaries, even to the point of rearranging them. He hypothesized a fluidity-rigidity dimension within these boundaries: certain boundaries will yield to influence and permit reaction; certain boundaries will resist influence and limit reaction. —We must keep in mind the Fixed and Mutable modes in Astrology.

Across the cell boundaries, one fact in the personality's environment affects a fact in another cell field. There is a quality of ease or difficulty in interchange ("permeability"). Boundaries are altered, added, or taken away depending upon the needs of the moment.

Interchange is accomplished by "locomotion and communication," resulting from an interaction of facts. The region representing a fact will be related to another region. *The tie between them,* over or through boundaries, *determines the value of the experience.* —Astrological aspects are the locomotion and communication between the House fields of experience. Mutability emphasizes

Example 1

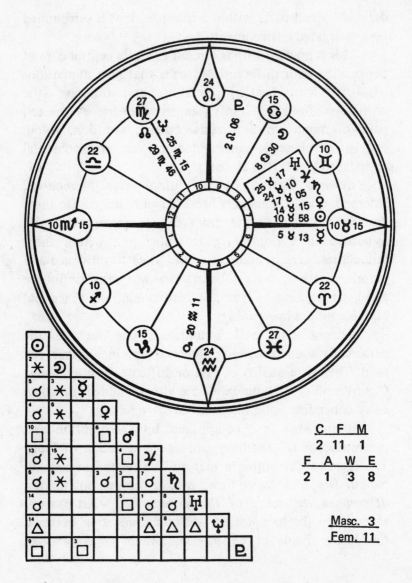

reaction; fixity resists it. The Cardinal influence supplies motivation for interchange. Rearrangements are made continuously in adapting to the environment. And within time—progressions and transits—these accumulated interchanges *alter* the cellular emphasis in the life space.

Lewin developed the field theory extensively to include *hodology*, the science of paths of locomotion and communication (aspects), and dimensions of reality and unreality, past and future. He studied the value of *tension* as the energy that invades the borders and originates interchange. Two or more tensions will push the personality into several directions, the result achieved from all the forces.

In example 1, a private case, page 8, astrological field theory shows a very debilitated personality. The young man is deeply anxious about personal relationships (Mars squares the House VII stellium). His communication ability is seriously hampered (Mars in House III; Mercury squares Pluto) to the point of a serious nervous stuttering. The personality is locked away in fears about his emotional security (Moon in Cancer in House VIII) yet functions well enough (Moon's sextiles with the Sun, Mercury, Venus, and Saturn) for him to maintain a job (in a physics laboratory).

He has lost the perspective of his personality in reality (Pluto squares Mercury and the Sun). His structure works against him, holds him within himself (eleven points Fixed; only the Moon and Neptune are in other modes). Analytically, the focus is upon his parents (Uranus and

Saturn ruling IV; the Sun ruling X; all related to Mars) and his emotional insecurity (somehow because of them) in public projection (House VII stellium; Sun exactly opposes the Ascendant). A deep sensitivity (eleven points feminine; only Mars, Pluto, and the Mid-Heaven are in masculine Signs) makes him temperamentally the victim of Mars, the "handle" of the bucket formation focused within the relationship quadrant. The whole Self is affected (Pluto and Mars rule the Ascendant, Scorpio, the Sign of self-destruction).

Viewing the horoscope in terms of field theory, we see that Mars in Aquarius (self-centered energy, to win the world for a friend) permeates the boundaries of cell VII, the House of the public, the planets in Taurus, public structure in this case. Tension vectors are created that press the native's life-energy (the Sun aspects every body in the horoscope) in upon itself; the tension vector of the mind (Mercury square Pluto, ruler of the Ascendant) complicates the communication, adjustment, and perception processes. The personality form performs in spite of the tensions: the Moon is positively related to the Sun, Mercury, Venus, Jupiter, and Saturn and is in its own Sign, Cancer ... yet it is alone in the emotional depths ... within cell VIII, with Gemini on the boundary, ruled by Mercury debilitated by Pluto.

Drawing this horoscope in field theory terms, the diagram shows strongly reinforced, rigid boundaries around the cells that are related by cell interchange (the aspects). (See page 11.)

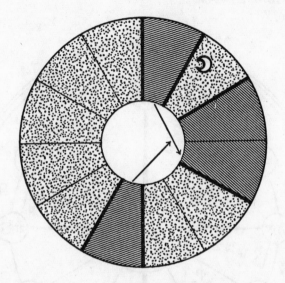

The cells (Houses affected are III and IX (the axis of the mind), VII, the public, relationships, and VI (Mercury position, Aries on VI ruled by Mars; Mercury's square with Pluto), sickness and the sense of work and service with others. The Moon, the personality form, is isolated between the two cells that are above the line of awareness (the horizon). The vectors of locomotion (the aspects) connect the cells and form a dissociated complex.

By rulership, the *entire* horoscope field is involved with this cell complex; the other cells become dotted with the trauma shade as well: Pluto rules I from IX, Jupiter rules II from VII, Uranus rules IV from VII; Jupiter has co-rulership of Pisces on V and is placed in House VII, Mercury rules VIII from VI, the Sun rules X from VII,

Example 2: Harry Weiss, "Houdini," magician
April 6, 1874; 2:24 AM
Appleton, WI

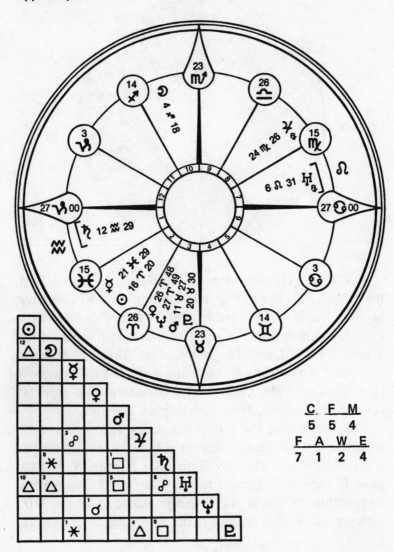

Mercury rules XI from VI, and Venus rules XII from VII. The entire personality is consumed by the dynamic trauma.

The native's behavior will be conditioned by this cell complex. The emphasis upon Fixed Signs is so extreme that the boundaries gain a tremendous rigidity. New cell formations for this young man might only be possible through psychomedical therapy.

Example 2 is the horoscope of Harry Houdini whose name has taken a place in modern mythology (see page 12). The incomparable showman, magician, illusionist, and above all, escape artist has a remarkable horoscope: a Grand Trine in the Fire Family (Moon-Sun-Uranus) and a powerful T Square among Saturn-Uranus and Mars in Fixed Signs.[3]

Houdini was a superb example of the Grand Trine in Fire: a closed circuit of inspirational self-sufficiency, individualism to the highest degree. The entire thrust of the ego, the personal worth (Sun in Aries in House II) received a tremendous, heroically arrogant public projection through Uranus in the Sun's Sign, Leo, in House VII and the Moon in Sagittarius in House X, ruler of Cancer on VII. Houdini challenged the world to stump him. He claimed that he could extricate himself from any confinement, any restraint, any bond. His showmanship rivaled his actual technical skill. The Sun-Moon blend from Volume III series reads: "independence gains an easy

3. The Grand Trine and T Square formations are fully explained in Volume IV of this series.

development through thought, action, speech, ideas, principles. The benefits of careful mental training can release wonders. The power of the Aries energy is directed to control the ideas and the minds of others. A terrific force of expression, social appeal."

The T Square was a tremendous complement to the Grand Trine since both figures shared a focus upon Uranus, ruler of Aquarius intercepted in the Ascendant. The power of this T Square is awesome.

> Saturn opposed Uranus: "independence loses touch with ambition's strategy."
> Mars square Saturn: nervous rebellion, clash, bad judgment.
> Mars square Uranus: "temper. Individual headstrong drive breaks social restraints. Independence ignores solid foundations."

The T Square synthesis would be toward powerful driving ambition, unique to the extreme, fighting for recognition, even to the extent of flaunting bad judgment and risk.

Histories of magic and magicians frequently refer to the Houdini temper, the extraordinary chances he took, defying the obvious bad judgment of a situation and breaking through incredible restraints to prove himself against certain death, i.e., chained and tied within a coffin, all encased within a nailed wooden box, lowered into an ice-covered river, only to escape, leaving the restraints behind him. —Houdini's entire image seemed projected to overcome the T Square through the Grand Trine.

The opposition between Mercury and Jupiter gave the dimension of exaggeration to Houdini's showman mind. The conjunction between Venus and Neptune in Aries, along with Mars and Pluto, in House III, gives us an indication of his enormous communication magnetism, the allure of illusion, his obsession with communicating with the afterlife, and his subsequent exposure of many false mediums.

When we view these fields of experience through psychological field theory as it can apply to the horoscope, the picture of personality is dramatic.

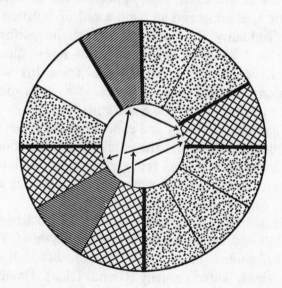

The entire organization of the personality is focused upon the House VII outlet. The eastern hemisphere orientation (ego) is controlled to and through the public. This public cell receives vectors of locomotion from Houses I, II, III, and X. By rulership, other Houses are involved as well: Venus rules IV and IX from III, Mercury rules V and VIII from II, the Moon rules VI from X, Saturn rules XII from I.

House XI (goals, wishes, friends, love received) is ruled by Jupiter in House VIII. Jupiter is in an awareness aspect with Mercury (exaggeration). House XI was relatively isolated from the main cellular organization. Jupiter was retrograde. There was a counterpoint within Houdini's enthusiasms, the opportunities he created: a wish for friendship and acclaim, a cell of isolation within the individuality of his fame and public performance. Biographical sketches by those who knew him reveal Houdini's tremendous dependence upon his wife for professional advice and guidance. We must note the extreme prominence of the Sagittarius Moon.

The fields of energy and experience show that the ego was projected mightily to the public. The motivation could well have been an isolated sense of loneliness, overcompensated through exaggerated conquering of the T Square, demanding public acclaim.

Houdini defied the world to trick him, believing in his own skill and endurance to overcome anything. This was bad judgment indeed (T Square) although it was incomparable entertainment (Grand Trine). Houdini died as a result of his bad judgment. On 30 October 1926, after a midday lecture on physical fitness, he exposed himself to body blows from the audience. He was alone, without his assistant who usually carefully arranged the feats, insuring Houdini's preparedness. A low blow caught Houdini unprepared, and he died the next day from a ruptured appendix. —At the moment of death, Mars, in its motion forty eight years and six months after Houdini's birth, had returned precisely to its birth position, and the Moon had just passed the birth position of Uranus.[4] The transits activated the bad judgment, explosive T Square. Houdini was caught alone, unprepared, the victim of the public he challenged.

In both horoscope examples, boundaries were established around cells of experience and behavior, emphasizing significance by isolating emphasis. Within Astrology, we can assume that the boundaries between trines and sextiles have high permeability, receive and transmit easily, with less tension. The boundaries between cells involved in squares and oppositions would be much stronger, much more tense, developmentally tense. The cells in Cardinal Signs would be motivational in behavioral experience; in Mutable Signs, reactant; in Fixed Signs, stolid, determined, unyielding. —Lewin refers to the dynamic properties of a region or cell (group) of the inner-personal sphere as a *system*. He maintained that tension within the system tends to equalize itself to the amount of tension in surrounding systems. The psychological means by which tension becomes equalized is called a *process*. The process is how one behaves, what

4. These planetary movements after birth are called *transits*. They are presented for study in Volume VII.

one does to find equilibrium. What others see and formulate within the process is called personality.

The process applies to the system as a whole *but not necessarily to all the parts-systems*. In the first horoscope example, ·through rulership, the *entire* personality *is* involved in the trauma; the cell system is in unyielding Fixed Signs. In Houdini's horoscope field, the focus was stolidly established in cell VII and, through rulership, involved the whole horoscope except for the House XI cell.

To gain equilibrium, a person will often take on tension with awareness that the result will be a more perfect balance of forces. We can say that Houdini took on the ultimate in tension, the restraints and threats of death, to command recognition of his ego . . . even to promising to communicate after death. The deep personal wish for love and acceptance (House XI) seems small and isolated in comparison with his monumental personality show. The isoloated cell XI was a private subsystem that motivated the whole and was fulfilled in part by his wife. At death, in a process of bad judgment, the tension toward equilibrium got out of hand. Discipline was left behind. The cells died.

Psychologists recognize that personality cannot exist without tension. Many claim that man works to make the tension as painless, as pleasurable as possible. Lewin especially saw systems of tension as *reservoirs of energy* for the psychological process. People who establish an equilibrium on a high-tension level differ noticeably from people who establish an equilibrium on a low-tension level.

—We can observe so easily in the study of the horoscopes of famous people how the overcoming of powerful tensions finally to achieve equilibrium establishes enormous achievement and fame. Conversely, low-tension horoscopes seem to "settle" into an equilibrium at a much lower level. The struggle with the variegated environment resolves the processes of tension. There are people (horoscopes) who thrive on tension. There are people who cannot—or think they cannot—tolerate even minimal tension. The cell complex involved in interchange with other cells symbolizes experiences coming together to challenge the system and its processes toward equilibrium. Restlessness is an indication that equilibrium has not been fulfilled.

The astrologer can observe this in many situations. For example, frustration is the manifestation of tensions not adequately expressed: a housewife who feels confined by her housework, perhaps more talented, more tense for progress than her husband; one individual in a group that has found its own equilibrium may not be individually satisfied and will disrupt group equilibrium, trying to express individual tension.

Behavior become the *reaction* to a *need. Need plus behavior equals personality.*

Needs. Lewin describes a need as an increase of tension or release of energy within an inner-personal region, a cell system. A criticism of the Lewin field theory is the apparent exclusion of birth endowment, family influence. Astrology, with its emphasis of birth endowment, *can* delineate need eloquently.

Needs motivate behavior and affect the formation of personality. The Moon is the symbol of the personality's form. When we study the Moon in a horoscope in its particular Sign, we gain an image of personality, how the Self is shown in behavior. All descriptions of the Moon in the Signs tell what the personality form *is*. Actually, analyses of the Moon in the Signs tell what the personality *needs to be*. Aspect formations within the horoscope may make this process of becoming extremely difficult (debilitating tension), challenging (developmental tension), or very easy (well supported). But the signification of the Moon defines the particular needs-to-become of the personality.

In our first example, page 8, the native had the Moon in Cancer: "senses and emotions will be heightened; the changeability will be less, having found security. The home will be very important, and the native will take himself quite seriously. Powerful intuitions give a self-assurance that is difficult to make understood by others. This position is meditative. Contentment can work against externalization .... The mother image is very strong." —This description tells what the native instinctively *needs*, ideally. Having unchanging security in the home, through the mother, taking it all very sensitively, privately, is what will bring the personality a core equilibrium. All work to resolve environmental and internal tensions will be directed toward gaining this primary personality equilibrium need.

The Moon is isolated in this example, in the meditative, emotional depths of House VIII. Its five sextiles gave the personality needs support enough to make a self-presentation within the severely debilitated whole horoscope. The focus upon House IV through the powerful squares received by Uranus and Saturn from Mars brought many vectors of tension to the subsystem of home and parental security. The whole horoscope was involved through rulership. The personality system became focused upon the heavily bounded cells; the dissociated complex demanded through its strength the establishment of equilibrium for the whole system. The personal needs were overpowered. The frustration was kept private, meditative, and affected communication seriously.

The German native is strongly attached to his mother, who worries herself about him and with him to the point of hysteria. The young man (born in 1941) still lives at home. His father was lost in World War II. His mother married a tyrannical, gruff man. The stepfather (Aries) took over the home. The mother and son cringe before the man still and, within national sociological traditions from a preceding generation, obey without voice. —Interestingly, the young man has three sisters who appear not to be affected by the situation. They are female, yes, and do not have the same identification problem with the stepfather, but their Moons are in different Signs. Their *needs* are different.

Houdini's elevated Moon (example 2, page 12) was in Sagittarius: "impressions not only gain focus, but they are elevated and propelled into public awareness. The intelligence is clear and extremely refined .... a loftiness of inspiration. Goals are sometimes too high for the energy." This was Houdini, whose enormous energy from the reservoir of tension within the T Square achieved public awareness, realization of inspiration, fulfilling extraordinary goal challenges. Houdini fulfilled his needs; his personality became monumentally clear. His Moon was superbly aspected within the Grand Trine and through a sextile with Saturn. Saturn related to Uranus (by opposition) within the Grand Trine; the Moon was elevated and placed in an angle.

The Sign of the Moon and its House position describe the reigning needs of the person within the process of becoming. The needs are modified by interchange (aspects) within the whole personal life space. The whole absorbs tension vectors from the variegated environment. The behavioral process strives for the realization of needs and equilibrium.

Behavior. Behavior is the activity stimulated to fulfill needs, to reduce tension. But tension does not always have to lead *directly* to action; a powerful aspect is often modified, re-routed by other aspects. The tensions may be synthesized and then action chosen by the mind to seek an equilibrium. The activity takes place in an experiential medium. Indirect action occurs when the personality *manipulates the environment,* reorganizes systems in order to achieve equilibrium.

The young german (example 1, page 8) sought to identify with authority figures to gain forceful expression, to discharge his tensions about personal sensitivity and security needs. He fell in with a neo-Nazi movement. His mind lost perspective (Mercury square Pluto). He vainly sought a rearranged environment, curiously still within an authority framework similarly represented by his stepfather.

Houdini manipulated his environment to an extreme and was successful. He engineered feats of ingenuity and inspired showmanship that are legendary. The reservoir of energy held within the T Square was constantly discharging through the inspired Fire Grand Trine. He was constantly escaping the threat of tension to create his own equilibrium . . . to the point of constantly risking his life.

Lewin suggests that, in addition to manipulating the environment, the personality can create *imaginary locomotions,* i.e., imagine the discharge of tension and enjoy vicariously an imagined equilibrium. This is the product of daydreaming; to an extreme, a psychosis, a departure from reality. When we see the aspects Mercury opposed or square Neptune, we know immediately that daydreaming and confusion are present in the personality. But that is not enough: we must give substance to the deduction; we must ascertain about what the personality daydreams, what is the native's imaginary locomotion, how it is related to the native's needs.

Neither of our examples was a daydreamer. Example 1 lost perspective almost totally through a fixation, tried vainly to manipulate the environment, but at all times appeared to be trying desperately to relate on others' terms within the experiences of relationships (hemisphere emphasis, Volume IV). Houdini created illusion and exploited the imaginary locomotions of his public. The public recognition of the impossible realized was his acclamation and reward.

Every person uses self-projection, self-motivation, imaginary locomotion to one degree or another. Finding out from a person the goals he sees for himself, his hopes—and, if developed, his daydreams—reveals much about that person's needs and his *ability* to satisfy them. The importance of this deduction grows with the age of the personality: age brings variety of opportunity and establishes a past record of behavioral achievement. Sometimes needs are regularly fulfilled, building more and more in accumulated success (Houdini); sometimes needs are regularly frustrated, strengthening the boundaries of frustration that isolate the painful cell systems (example 1).

Differentiation. For Lewin, differentiation was a key consideration in his theory of personality development. He defined differentiation as *an increase in the number of parts within the whole.* The adult has many more differentiated systems within his life space than the child has. Increasing maturity also refines the differentiation in a reality-unreality, practical-impractical dimension. With development, the person learns to distinguish between different degrees of possibility and probability. The person learns instinctively *to adjust his needs* within his awareness of his behavioral ability to establish equilibrium for them.

In Gestalt field theory, differentiation implies an increase in the number of cells, therefore an increase in the number of boundaries between them. Translating this into

Astrology, the House meanings gain a differentiation and greater subdivision, different levels of experience, to satidfy the needs of the personality form.

Equilibrium becomes a much more dynamic process: *integration*. The parts establish equilibrium through integration. The personality gains a richness of texture. Lewin suggests the operation of "organizational interdependence": the influence between cells is reciprocal and mutual. Being an artist (cell V) might make a man a better lawyer (House IX, trine) and vice versa; a banker (cell II) might use his financial skills to develop himself (square) as an art collector; the art collector may develop into a financial wizard within his aesthetic business.

Lewin's hypothesis of the increase in the number of cells is best translated into Astrology through the Derivative House System (Volume II), where any House except the Ascendant becomes the base House (Ascendant) for a derivative horoscope within the original.

In example 1, the fixation, the dissociated complex, is so extreme, affecting the whole horoscope, that derivative House reading is fruitless: the complex works against the differentiation of cells, experience, the increase of personality dimension. —On the other hand, Houdini's horoscope invites derivative House reading perfectly through the cell differentiation within a powerfully expanded life space. House VII is the House-cell of the wife: Uranus in House VII represents her primarily (as does the Moon, a feminine figure symbol, ruling Cancer on the cusp of VII; and the Sun, ruling Leo intercepted in VII; *all* within the Grand Trine). We begin with House VII as Houdini's wife's first. Jupiter retrograde in House VIII would be in his wife's second, the second of VII: his wife's strength behind the scenes, especially with attention to personal details (Virgo), would be a powerful influence upon Houdini's own sense of worth and his thinking process (opposition aspect with Mercury in House II in Pisces, co-ruled by Jupiter, mutual reception). Jupiter's trine with Pluto in House III, the ninth (higher senses, religion) of House VII, speaks definitely about Houdini's pledge to communicate with her after death. Houdini's House XI was the fifth of House VII: the love Houdini received from his wife, her creativity, her support of wishes for himself. Jupiter rules Sagittarius upon the cusp of XI.

For Lewin, the development of behavior is a function of the person within the psychological environment; man within his spatial order.

Summary

1. The way in which an object (experience) is perceived is determined by the total context or confguration in which the object is embedded. The personality's formation takes place within its reactions to personal needs and the demands of the environment. The whole is affected through interrelationship of the parts.

2. Cells of needs and experiences (Houses) are defined by boundaries with qualities of permeation. Tension vectors (aspects) permeate boundaries to establish interchange, locomotion, and communication.

3. Cell groupings function as systems of expression (aspects), motivating processes of tension equalization toward equilibrium. The cell groupings become reservoirs of energy for the psychological process.

4. Needs motivate behavior. The reigning need can be defined astrologically as what the personality form *needs to be,* seen through the Sign and House position of the Moon. Other needs follow in service to the reigning need (elaborated in chapter 3).

5. Behavior is manipulation of the environment, directly through action or indirectly through imaginary locomotion. The goal is to establish equilibrium tangibly or vicariously.

6. With age, experience, and maturity, differentiation takes place: cells of potential increase, the number of parts increases within the whole. Interchange becomes dynamic, reciprocal interaction among the parts. The full texture of personality functions within the psychological environment.

2

Attitudes and Functions

Carl Gustav Jung

Jung is often spoken of in the same breath with Freud. The two were colleagues and, in fact, Freud chose Jung to be his successor. However, their friendship was broken in 1913 in part because of Jung's rejection of Freud's concentration upon his own sexual theory. Their separation was total, and Jung went his own way to forge his analytical psychology. —We include Jung before Freud in this volume since Jung's theories are more accessible to understanding and observation within life and the horoscope field.

Carl Gustav Jung was born on 26 July 1875 near Basel, Switzerland (7:20 PM). He was a psychiatrist and philosopher, working in private practice exclusively after 1913. His papers and many volumes comprise a vast production. Only a few keynotes of his theories are presented here to illuminate from another direction techniques of analysis in Astrology. His major focus of investigation was upon the deepest lying processes of the human personality, the unconscious processes of the individual and of the human race, i.e., the collective unconscious.

29

Jung combined man's individual and racial history (as causality) with his aims and aspirations (as goal orientation). Both past *and* future guided behavior.

The collective unconscious conceived by Jung is the reservoir of memories inherited from man's ancestral past. We inherit the possibility of reviving experiences from this memory storehouse. Instinctive fears of the dark, acknowledgment of a god figure, and reaction to the mother are examples of the collective unconscious, the foundation for ego expression and personality development in life. Experiences bring concrete perceptions in the present together with images embedded in the past.

Archetypes are the structural components of the collective unconscious. Archetypes are the image powers behind behavior patterns. In his work with dreams, Jung found universal symbolic forms within man's unconscious that appeared to have direct relationships to common archetypes. He studied mythology—and Astrology—intensively to get closer to the origin of archetypal symbols.

One can submit that the horoscope itself is an archetype, a circle of completeness, god endowment, a potential of fertility through experiential impregnation.[1] The order of the timeless cosmic whole gains personal awareness within an individual horoscope. In esoteric Astrology, the trans-Saturnian planets can reveal

1. In his book *Psychology and Alchemy,* Jung developed a psychology of totality, the total unity of the Self, upon the mandala (magic circle) symbol.

dimensions of a vast prebirth unconscious, a karma, an identification with the genius of time.

Beyond the circle, two of Jung's archetypes evolved into autonomous dynamic systems with particular relevance to Astrology.

The persona. The persona is a mask worn by the personality. The persona becomes the public personality, the *Moon* in relation to *public expectation,* the role played by the personality in the working out of individual need interaction with the environment. Wearing of the mask is either comfortable or uncomfortable, calm or tense, productive or debilitating, depending upon aspects to the Moon.

The anima-animus. The anima is the feminine archetype within the male, and the animus is the masculine archetype within the female. They act as collective images to help motivate members of one sex to understand and appreciate members of the other. —Astrologically, the gender distribution of the planets (Volume IV) could be a measure of the anima and animus. The sensitive changeability of the Moon and its relationship with the public through the persona would focus the gender distribution balance within the personality's temperament. An overemphasis of the animus within a female could give rise to the Adlerian "masculine protest" (chapter 4); and overemphasis of the anima within the male could give rise to a feeling of inferiority (Adler) or a hypersensitivity.

Jung conceived two major *attitudes* or orientations in personality: *extraversion* and *introversion*.

There is a whole class of men who at the moment of reaction to a given situation at first draw back a little as if with an unvoiced "no," and only after that are able to react; and there is another class who, in the same situation, come forward with an immediate reaction, apparently confident that their behavior is obviously right . . . . the former class corresponds to the introverted and the second to the extraverted attitude.[2]

The extraverted type is characterized by outward energy, interest in events, people, and things, relationships with them and a dependence upon them. The environment is motivation. Extraverts prefer to reshape (manipulate) the environment in their own style. —Astrologically, extraversion applies more to the Fire and Air Signs than to the Water and Earth.

The introverted type is characterized by energy turned inward, a sense of "inner necessity." There is a lack of confidence in relationships. —Astrologically, introversion applies more to the Water and Earth Signs than to the Fire and Air.

2. C.G. Jung, *Modern Man in Search of a Soul* (New York: Harcourt, Brace & World, Inc.), p. 85.

Extraversion and introversion are not states of expression initially, i.e., not initially functions of planets. Rather, they are *attitudes, states of being* that appear predetermined within man through the Signs and the hemisphere emphasis. The attitude is all-pervasive. —Astrologically, we would seek measurement of these attitudes in the patterns of planets within the birth horoscope: the hemisphere emphasis east or north (inclination to introversion); west or south (inclination to extraversion). The radically extreme charts analyzed in Volume IV illustrate hemisphere emphasis and patterns that unmistakably show the attitudes of introversion and extraversion within the personality. It is interesting to note that, in world society, the peoples of the West generally adopt an extraverted life style and the people of the East prefer an introverted life style.

Retrogradation (and the hemisphere emphasis of retrograde planet groups is another indication of introversion. Planets within the element pairs Fire-Air and Water-Earth (and whatever retrogradation counterpoint accents there may be) blend in every personality to create a dynamic balance between introversion and extraversion. The measurement of elements within a horoscope shows balance or imbalance, or how one system compensates for a weakness in another system. Some areas of the horoscope (cell groups) will be introverted, perhaps, and others will be extraverted.

Jung saw the weakness of extraverts to be superficiality, dependency on making a good impression, and a lack of self-criticism; of introverts:

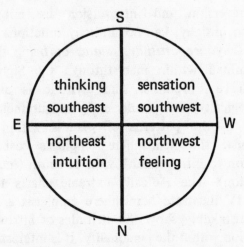

overconscientiousness, pessimism, hypercritical natures, easily misunderstandable. Although the two types tend to misunderstand each other, Jung saw a tendency for one type to marry the other. Each secretly hopes the other will compensate for the respective lack. The dangers are that one becomes critical of the other's values and a division occurs.

Jung postulated four fundamental *psychological* functions: intuition, sensation, feeling and thinking. —These are the symbolic descriptions given to each of the four quadrants of the horoscope in Volume IV: the northeast quadrant, intuition; the northwest quadrant, feeling; the southwest, sensation; the southeast, thinking.[3]

3. Sensation, the south-west quadrant, was called relation to avoid confusion with *feeling* during the introduction of the subject. Sensation was used by Jung in the sense of relating to experience.

Each attitude type, the extravert or the introvert, seeks to find its most developed function. Jung wrote that physical and mental health (balance) depends greatly upon development of any neglected function. With maturity (differentiation), people use more and more of every function. The life process is to reconcile the oppositions of these paired functions.

Example 3, page 36, is an example of the thinking type. Freud's horoscope immediately shows a powerful emphasis of the southeast, *thinking* quadrant. The extremely powerful T Square among retrograde Mars-Jupiter and Saturn includes within its outline every planet except Neptune. But Neptune (out of orb for the T Square) is square Saturn (and the Moon) independently. The opposition base of the T Square is in the parental, professional, home axis. With Mars in House IV and Saturn in square in House XII, we can deduce a severe, frustrating, privately terrifying problem with his father—and a positive, though stressful and perhaps ambivalent (Gemini) relationship with his mother (Mars trine the Moon, ruler of the Ascendant as well).

Mars and Venus are in mutual reception (Volume IV) and have a powerful bond in the same Zenith-Nadir axis. Mars and Venus are the only planets in Cardinal Signs.

A full analysis of this extremely demanding horoscope is out of place here. But the student should carry on with the theme that Freud sought to understand his own severe problems by forcibly unlocking the tension structures in others, especially through sexual self-understanding within an inhibited society (Mars in *Libra* retrograde, singleton).

Example 3: Sigmund Freud, psychoanalyst
May 6, 1856; 9:00 AM
Freiburg, Germany

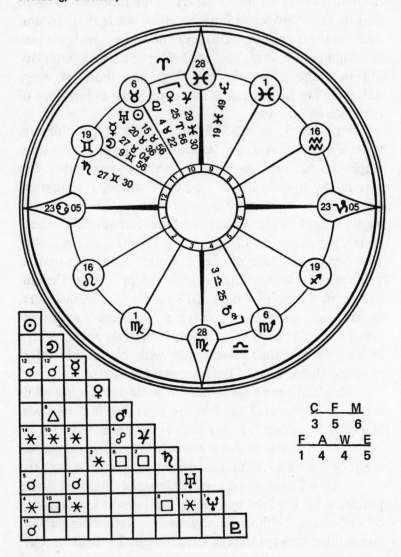

For a personality with the thinking function emphasized, according to Jung, conclusions are based upon objective data. The irrational is feared. The carefully formulated ends justify the means. Within the introverted type, an inner reality is sought. The weakness would be that the opposite feeling function would be undeveloped. —Freud was an introverted type: eastern hemisphere emphasis; Earth-Water emphasis; closure of the T Square including all planets except Neptune; Neptune square Saturn in House XII; singleton Mars retrograde as handle of the bucket, accenting the northern hemisphere powerfully.

Freud's enormous work was to give objective form to the unconscious, to formulate the irrational into the structure of scientific data. His genius for structuring the unconscious (Sun conjunct Uranus, Pluto, and Mercury in Taurus) justified his incisive probing (Mars) into the human mind. Sex became his cardinal theme, focused upon relationships within the family.

Freud's persona was his Moon in Gemini: the mind leading the emotions. The Moon was squared by Neptune: a dimension of unrealism and confusion. The trine with Mars saved Freud from deep personal mental sickness himself. His saving drive was to delve into the other side, the irrational that he himself feared. The feeling function was extrememly debilitated: Jupiter, ruler of Sagittarius on VI in the feeling quadrant was opposed by Mars, square with Saturn; Pluto was a safety, ruler of the creative, speculative, sexual House V and conjunct the Sun; Mars in mutual reception with Venus in its Detriment in Aries. The

Example 4: Richard M. Nixon, statesman
January 9, 1913; 9:44 PM, PST
Yorba Linda, CA

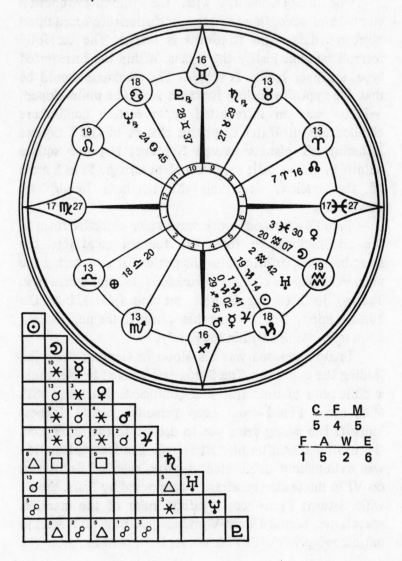

C F M
5 4 5

F A W E
1 5 2 6

retrogradation of the powerful singleton Mars within the T Square from an angle, in its Detriment, position in the feeling quadrant, accented crucially Freud's introversion and weakness in the feeling function. Applied energy (Mars) worked indirectly through professional counterpoint (ruler of Aries, intercepted in House X; retrograde).

The numerous sextiles gave his persona a functional ease that worked well within the Taurus structuring complex, organizing all the data objectively.

President Nixon's horoscope, example 4, page 38 (analyzed in Volumes III and IV), is a fine example of the feeling and thinking functions seeking equilibrium. The northwest quadrant (feeling) is powerfully emphasized. The Sun opposes Neptune and the House IV group opposes Pluto. These oppositions set up axes with the southeast quadrant. Neptune, Pluto (and Saturn) are retrograde and the only bodies above the horizon awareness line. The natures of these planets emphasize the thinking quadrant indeed and key us, through the retrogradation, the opposition aspects to the major group below the horizon in the feeling quadrant, to expect the functions to be expressed through the introverted type.

Jung described the feeling function as *separate from emotions.* The feeling function relies upon the *significance of the relationship* rather than the content. The extraverted type would be well adjusted to the world, sympathetic and helpful. For Nixon, through the indications that suggest the introverted type

Example 5: Edgar Cayce, spiritualist healer
March 18, 1877; 3:30 PM
Hopkinsville, KY

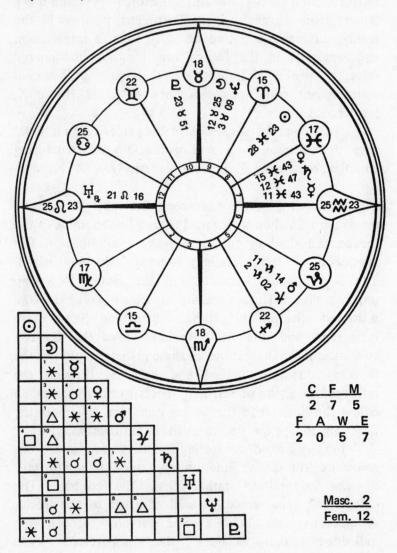

predominating (retrogradation, hemisphere emphasis, Earth-Water), subjective factors would become extremely important. He would appear cold, unadaptable, the depths beneath still waters.

Nixon's persona would be seen through his Moon Aquarius, strongly aspected with Saturn, ruler of the Capricorn Sun-Sign, and Pluto, opposing the House IV conjunctions: "humanitarian and religious instincts gain great importance . . . . the social theorist The objective at any level is to improve [social] situations . . . . grand service to the world" (Volume III). This is Nixon's image.

The powerful opposition aspect between Neptune retrograde and the Sun is the core axis between the thinking and feeling functions. Self-delusion and/or delusion by others (House XI: friends, public speculation as fifth of VII) would undermine the workings of the two functions. Saturn within the sensation quadrant (southwest) would structure ambition through relationships and experiences and support the Capricorn practicality. The intuitive function of the northeast quadrant is undeveloped, and Neptune, the planet of intuition, drains the Sun of its self-light.

Edgar Cayce's horoscope, example 5, page 40, illustrates emphasis upon the sensation function: the southwest quadrant is highly emphasized. The clairvoyant's Pisces Sun is within VIII, the House of occult and primal religious instincts. Uranus retrograde is upon the Ascendant and dominates the horoscope: the squares between Uranus, Pluto, and the Moon are the only major squares within the horoscope (Sun square Jupiter over the sign-line is not of major importance in this discussion). Enormous sensitivity is shown in relationship to other worlds, their message structured through Cayce into practical service: Uranus square to the Moon in Taurus from the Ascendant, Saturn in House VII, ruler of Capricorn on VI, Moon trine the Capricorn Mars; only the Ascendant and Uranus are in masculine Signs; the feminine, sensitive, anima emphasis is enormous.

The dominating Uranus retrograde upon the Ascendant and the House VIII position of the Sun would suggest a genius through introversion but not strongly enough for clear labeling. The square from the Moon to Uranus is the only major aspect made over the Zenith-Nadir axis between hemispheres, powerfully and singly linking Cayce's personality form with the core of selfhood, in a way of developmental genius. This tie between hemispheres is reinforced through the sextile between the Sun and Pluto. —Instead of an image of clear introversion, we must use the image of *passivity*. The Moon makes aspects with every body—another measurement of sensitivity—and only one, the square with Uranus, has developmental tension. All other aspects show an ease or a support within psychic (Piscean) focus. Cayce simply reacted, while in trance, to the sensations of his relationship with higher realms.

Jung describes the reliance upon the sensation function as pure acceptance, showing little logic. In the extraverted type, the object of the relationship would be more important than the actual sensation. In the introverted or passive type (Cayce), the substance of the sensation would dominate and be extremely difficult to understand.

Through rulership, the other functions are assimilated within the sensation quadrant, chiefly through Mercury and Venus in Pisces. This highly unusual man forsook almost all of life-experience to communicate with the beyond and serve mankind. He worked in a trance and never knew what had transpired.

His persona, the Moon in Taurus: "impressions are held with extreme obstinacy. The impression of self-contentment can overcome the personality .... the status quo too easily prevents progress and growth. Things are the way they are." —The congruence here with the emphasized passive sensation function is extraordinary. Cayce was fulfilling a unique role in the scheme of things.

His anima was extremely emphasized, with twelve points in feminine Signs, an exaggeration that corroborates his extreme sensitivity and passive attitude.

The entire horoscope reacted to the genius fixity of Uranus upon the Ascendant.

Look again at example 1, page 8: there is a high focus upon the sensation quadrant. The young man's personal needs, the role he wants to play through his persona Moon are in isolation within the field. His profile of introversion though accentuated by the power of the singleton Mars below the horizon is not enough (still in direct motion) to subdue completely his efforts to gain personal expression. The extraverted effort he does make suffers from the

Example 6

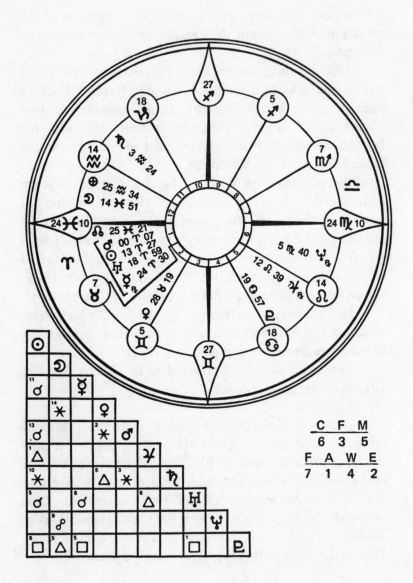

dissociated complex and the twisted mental perception.

Example 6 is a private case showing a powerful focus upon the intuition function, the northeast quadrant (page 44). The four planets in Aries within House I would promise intense individual projection, tremendous energy. However, the passive, reactant, Pisces Ascendant "waters down" the fire; Mercury is retrograde, suggesting a mental counterpoint, following the intuitive reaction nature of the Pisces Ascendant and Moon. The Pisces Moon is locked away within House XII and opposes Neptune retrograde, ruler of the Ascendant; the Sun is squared by Pluto, the Self is blocked, hidden.

This horoscope shows the intuitive function within an introverted type, totally unexpected from an Aries. —The man is very successful in his job as an industrial analyst: the Mars-Sun-Uranus conjunction trine with Jupiter, ruler of the Sagittarian Mid-Heaven. The Moon trines Pluto. Pluto and Jupiter within House V give a creative ease to the personality that gains respected position within large institutions easily. The man is a loner, an intuitive introverted type, who produces practical intuitive analyses easily.

Jung describes the intuitive function within the introverted type as visionary, benefiting from private perception, possibly a religious dimension.

The man's persona, the Moon in Pisces, a Don Quixote Moon: "the dream of truth and honor . . . . The personality is tuned in to inspiration . . . . impressionability. Private suffering corroborates known truths. Form is given to feelings."

Houdini's horoscope, example 2, page 12, shows the intuitive function within the extraverted type: the important things are the possibilities, the inspirations, the chances taken. Houdini's public awareness and professional application through the Moon in Sagittarius integrated the sensation and thinking quadrants well. The feeling quadrant was left interestingly undeveloped: Venus, ruler of Taurus, was in House III conjunct Neptune; the Moon, ruler of Cancer on VI, was in House X within the Grand Trine; and only Mercury, ruler of Gemini on the feeling House V, related the development of this function to where we know it must have gone: through the opposition with retrograde Jupiter to House XI in Sagittarius, the feeling House V for his wife, fifth of his House VII.

The four functions dictate how a person tends to react to experience. For example, a person stands before the pyramids of Egypt: if the intuitive function predominates, the person will react to the view in the sense of its grand mystery and eternal significance; if the feeling function predominates, the person will react in the sense of evaluated awe, size, and beauty; with the sensation function predominating, the tendency will be to react objectively, photographically; with the thinking function predominating, the tendency will be to understand the monuments architecturally, in principles and theory. Jung wrote:

A certain completeness is attained by these four. Sensation establishes what is actually given, thinking enables us to recognize its meaning, feeling tells us its value, and finally intuition points to the possibilities of the whence and whither that lie within the immediate facts. In this way, we can orientate ourselves with respect to the immediate world as completely as when we locate a place geographically by latitude and longitude.[4]

For any one individual, the least developed of the four functions is called the *inferior function* and is repressed and unconscious, expressing itself in dreams and fantasies. —Astrologically, the four functions are seen throughout the horoscope circle of completeness through the four quadrants. They focus upon the self-center, the point at the circle's center, the bisection of the horizon (line of awareness) and the Zenith-Nadir axis (line of experience). The circle of the horoscope with man at its center is the symbol of man's individual Sun: ☉.

The four functions and the two attitude types develop through a grand synthesis of astrological components (see page 48), beginning with the life-energy (the Sun); its Sign and placement within a quadrant; the attitude and functions highlighted by the development of a particular planet, applied through Mars through the role played by a particular planet, applied through Mars

4. Jung, *Modern Man*, p. 93.

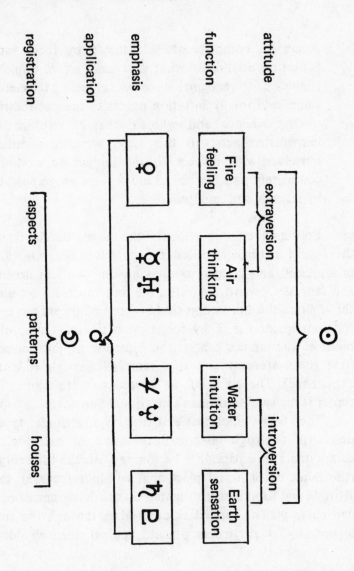

through the role played by the personality (the persona) serving the personal needs (Moon) in experience (the aspects, patterns, and Houses.

The most difficult function to distill is the feeling function, here associated with the Fire Family. Feeling is often confused with emotion. Feeling must be thought of as a *value* function, a subjective recording of pleasure and pain, anger, fear, sorrow, joy, and love. Jung makes the important point that *any* of the four functions can lead to *emotion,* but the emotion itself is not a *primary* function . . . it is a subjective response shared by *all* the objective functions of reaction. The feeling function is the reaction by which values are weighed, accepted, or refused for the Self (ego, Fire). The function is blended within attitude and specific energies of application. (Nixon's horoscope shows this clearly: the feeling quadrant is emphasized the the planetary pattern and the Sun's position, blended within the Capricorn attitude and expressed through the opposition aspects referring to other functions.)

The potential of *emotional response* permeates all four functions of the whole. The higher predisposition to emotional sensitivity would be seen in a predominance of the anima, an emphasis of feminine Signs; to rational coolness within emotions, seen in a predominance of the animus, the emphasis of masculine Signs.

Each person has all four functions, but they are not necessarily equally developed. The superior function usually gains one of the other three functions as an auxiliary, and the inferior functions suffer a repressed isolation.

Jung saw a compensation factor between the extraverted and introverted attitude types that organizes the four functions: when the extraverted attitude is thwarted within experience, the introverted attitude will rise in developmental importance. Astrologically, mood fluctuations within experience (the Moon) will occur, and different sections of the horoscope will speak more importantly in different situations. Frustration will bring introversion or extraversion to personality expression, normally of the opposite nature. The extravert will experience momentary introversion; the introvert will experience the need to break out, to express aggression through some kind of extraverison not typical of his normal behavior. Additionally, in a time of fulfillment, the extraverted portion of the horoscope will be pronounced in expression (pride); in a time when failure is felt, the introverted portion of the horoscope will be emphasized (diffidence, withdrawal).

There is a compensation factor between the polarities of function as well: when the thinking function is frustrated, the feeling function of evaluation gains ascendancy; when the sensation function is frustrated, the intuitive function gains emphasis. When a function is conspicuously undeveloped, the Self has nothing to fall back on.

In example 1, page 8, the young man rushes headlong into experiences (sensation) to establish personal relationships. The extraverted dimension (above the horizon) was constantly frustrated (square complexes) and his applied energy (Mars) would not serve the needs or fulfill the role of his persona (Moon isolation). The intuitive function (opposite quadrant) was underdeveloped by planetary position and reference rulership, yet it was sharply activated by the problematic singleton Mars. The native instinctively fears the compensation potential of intuition, i.e., that which would turn him inwardly toward his own painful problems. The fear of aloneness prods him even further into tense relationships. He has become fixed in his goal orientation and stutters in impotence.

Freud (example 3, page 36) had a tremendously overemphasized thinking function. (Note Mercury and Uranus in conjunction with the Sun as well.) The feeling function was underdeveloped but, similar to the first example, was insidiously accented by the retrograde Mars in Libra . . . the application of energy turned inward, in compensation, into the minds of others and their relationships, applying thought-out values to the fantasies of others. (Note that Mars and Neptune are the only planets in the western hemisphere, yet both are tied to Saturn in Gemini in House XII by squares.)

Nixon's horoscope (example 4, page 38) shows the highly developed feeling function (values weighed, accepted, or refused) and the contrapuntal accentuation of the thinking function (not only by quadrant but by aspects as well: Mercury opposed Pluto retrograde; and by rulership: Mercury ruling X, Moon ruling XI and square retrograde Saturn, Sun ruling XII and opposing retrograde Neptune). The extraverted attitude suffers turnarounds, and the accented introverted attitude rises to protect the Self.

The passivity of Edgar Cayce's horoscope (example 5, page 40) is unusual: he was in full relationship with other worlds, not simply through intuition (Jupiter trine Neptune, Neptune conjunct Moon), but through complete absorption by the paranormal situation of another world. His attitude was as a fixed medium, mutable receiver, experiencing life through an extraordinarily developed sensitivity dimension, anima (twelve points in feminine Signs). Note: Cayce's professional skill was as a photographer.

Jung believed—as do virtually all personality theorists—that a psychological theory of personality must be based upon a resolution of oppositions and tensions within conflict. Without such tension there would be no energy (developmental energy) and consequently no personality. In this sense, Cayce's horoscope comes close to having no personality of its own: the only developmental tensions are between the Moon and Pluto and their squares to the singleton Uranus upon the Ascendant in the Sign of the Sun, Leo.

In Jung's theory, the personality is pushed back and forth between the external demands of society and the inner demands of the collective unconscious. Within the struggle, the persona—or mask—develops. The personality is shown to the public. Astrologically, we can place the persona within the symbology of the Moon, as we have seen. The needs speak through various, changeable forms to gain degrees of acceptance. We can suggest that the role playing becomes less rigidly structured and more easily varied in form the closer the personality comes to fulfillment of its needs (Moon's Sign).

Jung believed that man is attempting to progress from a less complete stage of development to a more complete one, within a *partially* closed system of wholeness, open to influence from the environment and from the collective unconscious. The fulcrum of progress and development is again the function of the Moon between needs and experience.

The causes of development are twin stemmed, as we have seen: from the collective unconscious in the past (the needs) and the goals from the collective experience in the future. They meet within the present. Man's perspective must embrace both past and future, needs and goals, in order to avoid resignation as prisoner of the past and, subsequently, powerless in the fatalism of future experience. Proper perspective achieved through *compensatory development* of functions and attitudes gives man hope and an active role in effecting positive development. Man develops within a stable unity of his wholeness, an unfolding of the differentiated functions and processes of his personality's composition. The goal is to achieve the *transcendent function,* the realization, in all of its aspects, of the potential for wholeness crystallized at birth.

Summary

1. Both the past (racial history, collective unconscious) and future (goal orientation) guide behavior.

2. Archetypes, the structural elements of the collective unconscious, are the image powers behind behavior patterns. The *persona* is the behavioral role played, the mask worn by the personality (the Moon); the *anima* is the feminine component within man; the *animus* is the masculine component within woman.

3. Two major *attitudes* orient the personality: *extraversion* (outward energy and interests) and *introversion* (sense of inner necessity). Astrologically, extraversion: Fire and Air Signs, southern and western hemisphere emphases; introversion: Water and Earth Signs, northern and eastern hemisphere emphases, and retrogradation.

4. There are four fundamental psychological *functions:* intuition, feeling, sensation, and thinking, corresponding to Astrology's four horoscope quadrants. The four functions strive for balance, the superior function leading, the opposite (or inferior) function overcompensating when the superior function meets frustration. Negative tension triggers overcompensation between attitudes as well: between introversion and extraversion.

5. The drive in man is toward completion and transcendency: the fulfillment of self-potentials within past inheritance and future orientation, focused upon the dynamic, experiential present.

3

Needs

Henry Murray and Abraham Maslow

The concept of need is widely used in psychology. Needs are assumed and theories strive to establish their source, their intensity and interrelations, their expression and fulfillment. —Henry A. Murray, noted for his *personology* theory and the development of the Thematic Apperception Test, was born on 13 May 1893 in New York City. Also a physiologist and biochemist, Murray became an instructor in psychology at Harvard in 1927. During World War II, Murray worked for the Office of Strategic Services, analyzing candidates for complex, secret, and dangerous missions. He won the Legion of Merit award for his work and returned to Harvard in 1947 where he extablished the Psychological Clinic Annex for the study of personality.

Murray defines *need* as follows:

A need is a construct (a convenient fiction or hypothetical concept) which stands for a force . . . in the brain region, a force which organizes perception, apperception, intellection, conation and action in such a way as to transform in a certain direction an existing, unsatisfying situation. A need is sometimes provoked directly by internal processes of a certain kind ... but, more frequently (when in a state of readiness) by the occurrence of one of a few commonly effective presses [environmental forces] ...,. Thus, it manifests itself by leading the organism to search for or to avoid encountering or, when encountered, to attend and respond to certain kinds of press .... Each need is characteristically accompanied by a particular feeling or emotion and tends to use certain modes ... to further its trend. It may be weak or intense, momentary or enduring. But usually it persists and gives rise to a certain course of overt behavior (or fantasy), which ... changes the initiating circumstance in such a way as to bring about an end situation which stills (appeases or satisfies) the organism.[1]

Needs make things happen. The tensions of development reflect the meeting of needs and environmental demands within experience. The personality develops in relation to the measure of success and failure of need satisfaction. —For Astrology, the Moon in its Sign tells us the reigning needs of the individual. The Leo Moon needs authority; the Libra Moon needs harmony and social acceptance; the Capricorn Moon needs recognition and success in administration of the will, etc. The changeability

1. Calvin S. Hall and Gardner Lindzey, *Theories of Personality* (New York: John Wiley & Sons, Inc., 1957), p. 172.

of the Moon (its speed) provides a measure of the different roles assumed and the fluctuations of intensities during the fulfillment of needs. The aspects made with the Moon further modify the need profile, and the House position of the Moon determines the experiences within which the drama of need fulfillment is principally played.

Murray states that the existence of a need can be deduced on the basis of the following: (1) the effect or result of behavior (past record); (2) the particular pattern or mode of behavior involved (element and mode); (3) the selective attention and response to particular classes of stimuli (House); (4) the expression of a particular emotion or affect when achieved or frustrated (aspects).

Murray suggests different types of needs. We must view these astrologically as support needs for the reigning need established by the Sign and House positon of the Moon. These support needs work to fulfill the reigning need.

- Primary (*viscerogenic*) needs refer to organic and physically satisfying needs (and supporting experiences). Secondary (*psychogenic*) needs are derived from the primary but are less specific in focus: the primary needs of nutrition, sex, shelter give rise to the secondary needs of acquisition, dominance, construction, for example.
- Overt needs are expressed in actual motor behavior. Covert needs are expressed in fantasy, dreams, or displacement. Covert needs are usually at odds with society's restrictions.

- Focal needs have specific reference to specific environmental and experiential situations. When the attachment is firm, a fixation forms that can be debilitating (pathological). Diffuse needs lack enduring focus upon specific goals, and can also be debilitating.
- Proactive needs originate from within the personality. Reactive needs result from something originating within the environment.
- Modal needs emphasize the process of doing something; the attempt to achieve fulfillment exists as a need in its own right; talking too much, for example, gives a modal, functional pleasure to some. —Effect needs lead to some desired state or result.[2]

Houdini, example 2, page 12, had his Moon in Sagittarius, highly elevated, within the Grand Trine, and sextile Saturn (supporting ambition). Houdini's need to project himself (his personality) into public awareness was extremely accented in his horoscope. We could say that the reigning need was indeed primary, *viscerogenic*. His escapes were life-and-death matters, dependent upon superlative physical condition. (Sagittarius significance with exercise, sports, training.) The secondary need evolved from this to challenge the world and death to prove his inspirational self-reliance.

His showmanship (Moon in Sagittarius, Sun in Aries,

2. *Ibid.*, pp. 175-176.

Uranus in Leo in House VII) became his overt need: to project himself before the public. The covert need was to achieve immortality in a death-defying claim of personal excellence.

The containment of the Grand Trine and the Fixed T Square both focused upon Uranus in a Fixed Sign: his grand need was fixed to the point of mania. Without outlet, the need structure would have inverted pathologically. Houdini was a blend between the proactive needs within himself and the challenge needs he created among the public. The motor vitality was exploited to a physical extreme (the discharge of the T Square tension-energy reservoir).

His motor drives became modal needs in support of the grand, reigning scheme of personal projection. They led to fulfillment through effect needs—and to his death.

Murray recognizes instances where the outcome, the goal, of different needs is behaviorally the same: the *fusion* of needs; and the *subsidiation* of needs, where one or more needs serve the same reigning need. Houdini's horoscope illustrates this perfectly.

In a horoscope with Pisces or Gemini on the Mid-Heaven, especially, the astrologer faces the potential of duality within the personality, and usually of more than one profession. The whole horoscope will speak of different needs in different directions. The fusion of needs will be departmentalized; the subsidiation of needs will be divided; the House levels of experience will be highly differentiated. The multiple divisions will usually unite within the reigning need. —A government official is also a lawyer and author (Nixon, Gemini Mid-Heaven), Moon in Aquarius; a whiskey importer, diplomat, and politician (Joseph P. Kennedy, Gemini Mid-Heaven), Moon in Virgo; actor-politician (Ronald Reagan, Pisces Mid-Heaven), Moon in Taurus.

Just as the concept of need represents the determinants of behavior within the person, so the concept of *press* represents the determinants of behavior in the *environment*. The press of an object is what it does to or for the personality. Murray lists many presses: family insupport (discord, discipline, absence, illness, unsettledness): danger or misfortune (aloneness, darkness, water, height, fire, accident, animals); lack or loss (possessions, companionship, nourishment, variety); rejections; dominance; affiliations; sex; deception or betrayal; inferiority . . . and many others. —The *aspects* made by the Moon would show the *press* upon the personality and its work to fulfill individual needs: the sextile and trine would show support and ease within environmental press; the conjunction would intensify the basic need system; the square and opposition would bring developmental tension and polarized awareness to the need construct. *The aspects would refer to particular experiences and energies through the House position, Sign tenancy, and rulership of the aspecting planet.*

Edgar Cayce (example 5, page 40) had his Moon in Taurus. His need was to accept and structure things as they were, for public benefit. In House IX, the needs were within higher thought and mind activity, religion, ethics. In conjunctions with Neptune and Pluto, the needs gained a dimension of vision, other worldliness. The Moon sextiled Venus, Mercury, and Saturn in Pisces in House VII: mental vision was communicated easily, sympathetically, and wisely to the public; the Moon trined Mars and Jupiter in Capricorn in House V: he administered his visions well through creative channels. The only square, developmental press, was with Uranus upon the Ascendant: the genius dimension of otherworld communication at the core of his being. The press was to communicate through his own personality structure (Moon in Taurus), fulfilling his highly unusual potentials.

In example 1, page 8, the needs of the personality form were in isolation while the enormous presses within the environment raged.

In Nixon's horoscope, example 4, page 38. the Moon in Aquarius in House VI (humanitarian service needs) is square with retrograde Saturn in Taurus in House IX: the press upon the need is for conservative building, strategic economy, prudence, and patience; all within an international framework.

Theoretically, each planet in the horoscope will represent a need of its own in the dimension of the planet's nature and House position. Mercury will suggest the needs of the mind; Venus, the needs of the emotions and the aesthetic sense; Mars, the needs for energy expression; Jupiter, the religious, ethical, and opportunity needs; Saturn, the needs of ambition; Uranus, the needs of individuality; Neptune, needs of vision, dream life, the unconscious (chapter 5); Pluto, the needs within public perspective. —The synthesis of the horoscope relates the support needs to the reigning need symbolized by the Moon.

Murray postulates a concept of *sentiment*, representing a different way of viewing the same phenomenon, an "enduring disposition to respond." Astrology can absorb this within the Cardinal, Fixed, and Mutable Modes. The Cardinal emphasis will embody the master motives that initiate action to serve the need; the Fixed emphasis will embody a complex structure that will tend to preserve the status quo and protect each step toward fulfillment; the Mutable emphasis will embody the means of expediency, the means of change and adaptability toward fulfillment of needs.

Murray suggests that an individual learns not only to respond to press in a manner that will reduce tension (through fulfillment) but also to respond in a manner that *develops* a tension that will gain quicker fulfillment and be reduced later. This recalls Lewin's premise that man will often take on tension (accept responsibility, challenge, change) with the awareness that the result will be a more perfect balance of forces. —Astrologically, a person may invite change and tension to challenge the system to higher fulfillment of personal needs . . . or see tension as a challenge and opportunity. Adaptability and anchored focus would be the best attributes with which to take on such extra stress (Houdini).

Murray's personology theory goes deeply into

measuring the ramifications of needs. He is a psychologist who assigns a major developmental role to environmental factors (press) and a lesser role to psychoanalytic factors within the person. His ideas recall the differentiated life space and increase of cells in the field theory. Murray, by his own admission, was deeply influenced by Jung, and the role position of the personality, the "need for roleship" within environmental interaction certainly describes the persona vividly. He includes psychoanalytic theory through an exposition of covert and overt needs, the former imbedded within the unconscious. However, his emphasis upon the socialization process channels the reduction of need tensions into a flexibility and malleability of the personality, an *alteration of the person himself within environmental press.*

Abraham Maslow is chairman of the department of psychology at Brandeis University. He criticizes psychological theories for negative and limited conceptions of man. He deals particularly with the well-being, the wholly positive side of personality expression. Maslow asserts that man has an inborn nature that is essentially good, never evil. The novelty of this theory when it was introduced was that most psychological theories assumed that man's instincts and motives were bad and must be trained through socialization.

Maslow maintains that man becomes wicked, miserable, or neurotic only because the environment has made him so. In other words, man becomes negative when his needs are not fulfilled in good enough measure by his interaction with the environment. As soon as frustration is removed, aggression disappears. —Or conversely, one may add that as frustration is induced, aggression appears.

Maslow's motivational theory is based upon a hierarchy, *a priority or potency of needs.* He suggests that needs follow a hierarchal order from the need of the greatest potency to the need of the least; when the stronger need is fulfilled, the next need upon the scale asserts itself and demands fulfillment. The order begins with the physiological needs such as hunger and thirst, then the safety and shelter needs, needs for belonging and love, next esteem needs, needs to know, and then aesthetic needs. Each need, beginning with the first, takes precedence over one that follows in the order.

Companion to the hierarchy of needs was a profile embodied in well-adjusted persons. Maslow conducted an intriguing experiment: he gathered subjects that included many friends, colleagues, and personalities like Lincoln, Jefferson, Thoreau, Beethoven, Franklin Roosevelt, etc. He deduced that the factors, the well-adjusted profile, that separated this sample from the ordinary run of people were as follows:

1. Superior perception of reality.
2. Increased acceptance of self, of others and of nature.
3. Increased spontaneity.
4. Increase in problem-centering.
5. Increased detachment and desire for privacy.

6. Increased autonomy, and resistance to enculturation.
7. Greater freshness of appreciation, and richness of emotional reaction.
8. Higher frequency of peak experiences.
9. Increased identification with the human species.
10. Changed (the clinician would say, improved) interpersonal relations.
11. More democratic character structure.
12. Greatly increased creativeness.
13. Certain changes in the value system.[3]

These distinguishing features of the happy, wel-adjusted person show a superb awareness of individual position within the environmental field, the means of living with others and within press, and *a sincere responsiveness to opportunity* and challenge. Astrologically, these are the trines and sextiles that support the personality within the developmental tensions of personality emergence. It is important to note that few of these distinguishing features could exist if there were *no* personality tension, no challenging opportunity for their deployment. Maslow's well-adjusted profile is an index of reactions to tension.

Maslow's hierarchy of needs refers to a continuum of needs *that all persons share:* the physiological needs, the safety needs, the self-actualization needs, the aesthetic

3. Abraham H. Maslow, *Toward a Psychology of Being,* second edition (Princeton: D. Van Nostrand Company, Inc., 1968), p. 26.

Example 7

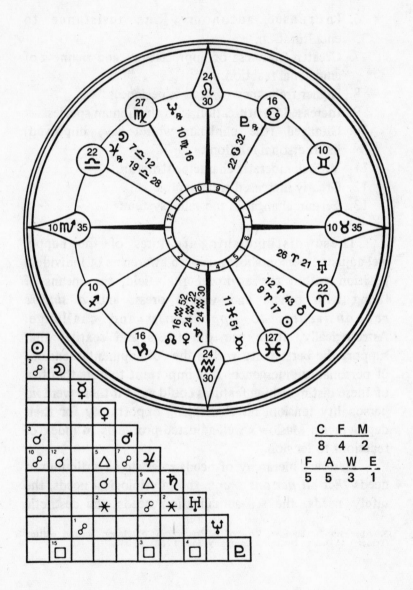

needs, etc. Astrologically, the Moon's position and aspect condition will represent the reigning need embracing special dimensions that work toward fulfillment.

In actual practice, the native's profitable recognition of the hierarchy of needs is well illustrated in example 7, a private case, page 66, the horoscope of a male restaurant owner: a Full-Moon birth, the Sun in Aries and Moon in Libra. The opposition between Mercury and Neptune retrograde (day-dreaming) overpowers the horoscope: the only planets in Angular Houses, the planets in mutual reception. The mind and its professional application—through the powerful Aries energy thrust—would be self-deluding, camouflaged somehow.

The opposition of the Moon and the Sun includes the opposition of Mars and Jupiter: a loss in gambling, violations of trust among friends—with a counterpoint (Jupiter retrograde)—perhaps concerning sex, Mars in Aries, Sun and Mars within the opposition, placed in House V.

The Scorpio Ascendant again keys us to the emotional depths . . . and we note that only Neptune is in an Earth Sign . . . camouflaged practicality. Pluto, ruler of the Ascendant, is square Jupiter (a philosophical tension with the ways of the world) and widely square the Moon.

The Moon is in Libra, ruled by Venus which is confined somehow by conjunction with Saturn in Uranus' Sign Aquarius. Uranus squares Pluto: "individualism is given spiritual rationale for reform." —The Moon is the only planet not retrograde above the horizon. There is a seesaw tension between the feeling and thinking quadrants.

The power of this Aries—highly focused by the conjunction with Mars—is diffused somehow, morally, ethically, individualistically, through friends; and camouflaged within the professional position, sexually, threatening personal emotional limitation (Venus rules Libra on XII). —The native is a homosexual, maintaining a superb restaurant as a home and working place for himself and his lover. The relationship has lasted some fifteen years.

The Moon in Libra will define the man's reigning need: "a Cinderella position," in which aesthetic perceptions must be satisfied and the personality is reflected through social relationships; the self-image requires refinement and grace and has the need to be regarded as charming. —The Moon is under tension through opposition with the Sun and Mars in Aries. The individual is fighting to command his own position but needs the unusual relationships, the refined milieu, the charming friends to balance him.

The native's support needs are complex: he needs the fine things of life, the foods, wines, friends and emotional freedoms in order to fulfill individuality. Yet, the dominating axis is Mercury-Neptune. His mind cannot apply itself as well as the Aries Sun wishes. It gets detoured by the enormous pull of the emotional and social needs. —Investment opportunities pass him by; salesmen opportunize him; his staff loses respect; frustrations mount; arguments with the lover (Libra Sun, Aries Ascendant) are bitter. The whole personality works to serve the need for balance. The Self never gets a chance to speak, to evaluate new situations, to apply progressive energy.

The man shares the same primary and secondary needs as all men, and he has satisfied them: he has built a beautiful dwelling, financial security, a social showplace, the finest self-nourishment. The reigning needs are satisfied; the *subsidiating* needs (Murray) ascend in importance; they press the personality with great urgency. The little things get out of hand. Things assumed, or overlooked before become focal centers. Tiny disagreements become love quarrels. Introversion overcomes the applied energy potential. —Conversely, if his business were threatened, his clientele diverted, his lover gone, the *primary needs* would once again gain ascendancy and the man would be *forced* by his own organism to see to their restoration in order.

The native's primary needs were well satisfied. The supporting needs were coming into prominence of their own: the Mercury-Neptune axis supported his covert needs and daydreaming replaced active fulfillment and the expression of overt needs; focal needs toward specific goals gave way to diffuse needs without specific goal orientation; the proactive needs within the personality became very strong and overcame the balancing reactive needs which grew traumatically tense; most obviously, needs that had been modes of support for the *higher needs* (the system supporting the reigning need) had become statically overemphasized. —The man is in superb social and professional fulfillment. The major needs are fulfilled. The lower-level needs rise to demand more attention on their own and become problematic. He daydreams of further investments in restaurants but cannot tear himself away from the relationship problems that have come into focus between him and his lover. Overall, his goal focus for living, for further personality development was lost.

The advice to this man was based upon Maslow's hierarchy of needs and Murray's personology. In phase with progressions and transits for the time ahead (Volumes VI and VII), the man was urged to break the long-term, now quarrelsome relationship with his lover (and employee), *to forcibly create a vacuum in his life.* The vacuum would leave needs unfulfilled, needs particularly pressing to the native. He would find a more realistic orientation, a clearer acceptance of himself and others; his energies would be keyed to spontaneous application; he would become problem-centered rather than self-centered; he would gain independence and privacy and a fresh appreciation of his fine professional and social position; his philosophy would gain perspective; his creativity and individuality would have more dynamic meaning. —The counsel stimulated far-reaching plans within the native: removal eventually to a foreign country, the restaurant maintained as a profitable investment, a building anew.

In a further dimension, it was deduced and corroborated that, within the love relationship over the many years, the native was forced into the passive role by the Libra mate (with Aries Ascendant). The native's own Aries power—his animus—had been totally subdued to keep the peace (note: masculine ten, feminine four).

Often in astrological counsel, the work is chiefly a

sorting out of variables, concerns, options—*needs* within time and a personal frame of reference. *When the hierarchy is upset, energy is awakened.* Strategic direction of energies within time builds adjustment with the environment and works to satisfy the individual's needs. —First things first!

We have studied the law of naturalness (Volume IV), the tendency toward cohesion of the parts within the whole. The level of a horoscope is established chiefly through a person's choice of goal, or profession. What a person wants out of life, what he does for a living key the level of the horoscope. Then, all the parts—the planets, the aspects, the House meanings—can be studied in relation to the level: different in focus for an airline pilot than for a doctor. —*Establishing level means discovering needs.* Discovering the needs of the organism (personality) means the establishing of a hierarchy of organismic functions to serve those needs. *Establishing needs means discovering level.* Neptune, for example, functions for both the artist and for the executive, but an individualized hierarchy of needs utilizes, expresses Neptune differently according to the needs and their value order with personality level.

Example 8, a private case, page 72, is the horoscope of an international bullfighter, a matador, who fights bulls in South America and Spain. He is a full *matador de toros,* who has received much international publicity.

In anticipation, one would expect measurements of bravery and power from Mars, perhaps a prominence of Taurus. One would least expect a diffusion of energies or

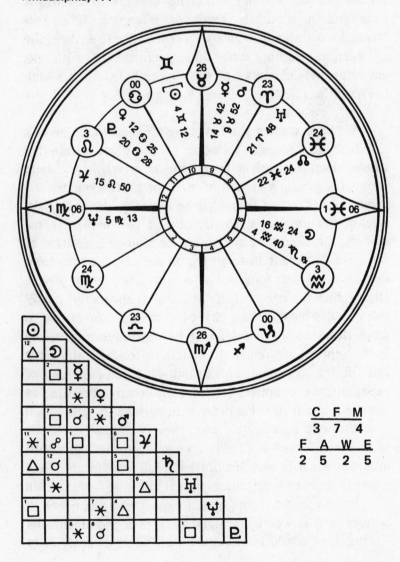

Example 8: John Fulton, matador
May 25, 1932; 12:22 PM, DST
Philadelphia, PA

the prominence of Neptune, for example. —The matador is a Gemini with the Sun square Neptune; Venus is conjunct Pluto in Cancer. Venus, as ruler of the Mid-Heaven and Libra on III gains importance. Mercury—in Taurus—gains special importance through elevation and rulership of Gemini in House X and the Virgo Ascendant.

Research of the birthdates of fifty-six of Spain's foremost bullfighters in history reveals that nine were Capricorn, nine were Aquarius, seven were Pisces, six were Sagittarius, six were Taurus, and the rest were distributed among the remaining Signs. Only two were Geminis. Manuel Rodriguez, "Manolete," who became a modern legend in Spain, was a Cancer. El Cordobes, *the* matador of the 1960s, has the Sun in the last degree of Taurus. —No pattern seems to emerge.

Studying books about bullfighting and seeing many *corridas* reveals that the arena is not so much a battleground as it is a stage. The *corrida* itself is not so much a fight as it is a staged drama. The drama is art more than it is struggle. A matador's horoscope would need the bullfight to express something more than sport or entertainment. The bullfight is a medium for personal expression of many kinds.

Bullfighting is a highly evolved, intensely developed modal need through which more primary effect needs are realized. The matador may have tremendous needs for big business and personal security (Manolete had the Moon in Capricorn)—matadors are the highest paid athletes in the world. He may have a tremendous high-priority need for unique artistic expression (our example)—the bullfight is balletic and painterly to the extreme. He may have a need to prove himself at all odds, to overcome inferiority feelings (Cordobes has the Moon in Taurus also, impoverished upbringing, Mercury retrograde in Gemini). Manolete became a legend for his almost melancholy stillness, his innovation of subtle passes. Cordobes (Moon in Taurus) is criticized for not bringing anything new to the art; applauded for his reckless courage.

In our example horoscope the Moon is in Aquarius. The matador's reigning need is humanitarian in nature, projected to the world unusually. His goals are to make a public impact uniquely. The modal and effect needs rose in more than one area of his professional life (Gemini Sun in House X). He is an author of several bullfighting and children's books. He is an acclaimed painter and illustrator with his own gallery in Seville. He was a fencing champion. He is the only American to have "taken his *alternativa*"—gained formal recognition as *matador de toros*—in Spain.

Studying the horoscope as that of an artist clarifies the picture. The Gemini Sun squares Neptune rising in the Ascendant, ruler of the public House VII; Venus is in conjunction with Pluto, sextile Mercury, ruler of the Ascendant and Sun-Sign . . . and Venus is sextile Mars; Mercury and Mars are in Venus' Sign, Taurus. The T Square among Jupiter, Moon-Saturn, and Mars-Mercury in Fixed Signs does introduce the reservoir of energy, the courage, the gamble, the personal drive toward fulfillment of the humanitarian needs, and the threat of bad judgment.

Saturn is retrograde and also in Aquarius. There is a counterpoint within his service ambition. Saturn is trine with Sun and rules Capricorn on V, creativity, children, theatricality. His ambition would have a secondary level involving the public projection of his unique creativity. —Additionally, he has adopted a Spanish gypsy boy who is an internationally recognized art prodigy.

The T Square energy releases itself into two distinctly separate directions: Mars is trine to the artistic Neptune, and indirectly to the Sun through the Mars square with Saturn. —The caution with the horoscope would be for accumulated bad judgment not to catch up with progress through the demands of the dual professions (Gemini in X).

The horoscope is summed up in the matador's own words (correspondence with the author):

I can only say that my interest in bullfighting, aside from the basic emotional appeal is an artistic interest. As a participant, it serves as a physical vehicle for artistic expression. Artist-matador: it is one and the same. —I am not the stereotyped magazine glamour type of matador. In the first place, I have never starved in my early childhood—so there are none of the poverty, salvation motivations bringing me to the arena. Through my bullfighting, my art work has been brought to the attention of more people than I could have hoped to reach otherwise.

In deep analysis of this horoscope, each planetary position and aspect would have to be read one way for the bullfighter and another way for the artist. The hierarchically prominent need for unique public presentation would embrace the division within the profession. For example: Neptune would be the artistic theatricality for the matador and the artistic vision for the artist . . . both under developmental tension with the versatile, adaptable, and cerebral Gemini Sun. The Venus conjunction with Pluto signifies "emotional projection to the masses or emotional downfall through emotional excesses" (Volume III). The conjunction is positively aspected through sextiles with Mercury and Mars and Neptune. (The square between Uranus and Pluto is a generation-background of spiritual rationale given to individualism.) The aesthetic in this horoscope would be linked with the masses (Pluto) as a goal of life (House XI). The aesthetic would be linked with both professional constructs (Sun-Neptune vision and T Square risk energy). In a Freudian dimension (chapter 5), with Pluto ruling Scorpio on IV (the end period of life as well as a new beginning), the Venus-Pluto conjunction in House XI would be interpreted as a deep death-wish . . . perhaps for one career to end and the other to gain ascendancy.

The functions of the planets and the House meanings in this horoscope are keyed to the two different levels established professionally. The levels are bound together within one dominant need: to project the unique personality to the public. The aesthetic gains strong relationship with the need center since Venus and Pluto are in Cancer, the Sign ruled by the Moon; Mercury, Mars, and the Mid-Heaven are in Taurus, ruled by Venus, the Sign of the Moon's exaltation.

When the personality's needs do have a duality, the psychological danger is that the functions will become exclusively separate, i.e., a split personality. However, it is by far the norm that the two or more professions, distinctly different, are *wedded within one reigning need:* "Artist-matador: it is one and the same." The person may be a writer and public performer within the dominant need to communicate. —The matador's horoscope shows an emphasis of the southern hemisphere, a dedication to experience, anchored below the horizon to personal vision and a unique sense of service-work projection to the world. The persona plays several roles to fulfill a singular need. Extraversion is well balanced with introversion. The thinking and sensing functions are well balanced through rulerships within aspects with the feeling and intuitive functions. The matador John Fulton is an extraordinary human being, a renaissance man.

Summary

1. Needs make things happen. The reigning need of a personality is seen through the Moon within the horoscope.

2. There are many types of needs: primary organic needs, secondary related needs, overt needs, hidden needs, focused or diffused needs, individual or environmental needs, modal or effect needs.

3. The needs (the reigning need and the subsidiary, supporting needs) interact with the environmental press. The tension increases to fulfill the need. The person himself changes to accommodate the changes in pressing tensions.

4. There is a hierarchy of needs that inclines to a well-adjusted profile when the needs are satisfied in good measure.

5. All persons share the same basic hierarchy of needs, but the hierarchy is typed, identified by the special need dimensions of the individual personality (and the reigning need). —When the hierarchy is upset, when priority needs require or lose fulfillment, tension is created and activity occurs.

6. Duality within the level of the horoscope establishes parallel branches of psychological and astrological functions, usually tied together within the reigning need. The parts of the personality, the horoscope, order themselves naturally around two themes of development within the greater whole.

4

Superiority and Inferiority

Alfred Adler

Consciousness is the center of the personality according to Adler—a view completely antithetical to Freud's with its emphasis on the unconscious center. For Adler, man is primarily a social creature. Man's reigning need is a *will to power*.

Alfred Adler was a psychiatrist. He was born in Vienna on 7 February 1870 and came to the United States in 1935 to serve as professor of medical psychology at the Long Island College of Medicine in New York. He died two years later, but his theory of personality development had long made its mark through his one hundred books and articles.

Adler assumed that man was motivated primarily by social urges, that he was *inherently* a social being. Freud (chapter 5) emphasized sex, Jung emphasized primordial thought patterns and inborn functions, and Adler stressed social interest. He formulated a concept of the creative Self that searches for experiential fulfillment of needs. The person creates a unique style of life to gain self-fulfillment, seeking out experiences or creating them.

79

Adler differed from Jung in that he said man is motivated *more* by his expectations of the future than by his experiences of the past. Man embraces *fictional finalisms* to guide his development into the future. These fictional finalisms are shared by many and help men deal more effectively with reality. For example: all men are created equal; honesty is the best policy; the end justifies the means; it's written in the Bible; it ain't necessarily so; all's well that ends well . . . these finalisms can exercise strong influence on personal behavior. —In extremes, these fictions can dominate a personality and create goals and needs to fulfill them that are too often beyond the reach of the personality. The fictionalized goal or style of life can be beyond the abilities shown in the horoscope: frustration replaces reward. The fictionalized goal or style of life can be much lower in level than the abilities shown in the horoscope: underachievement replaces progress.

The fiction can totally dominate the personal need hierarchy and mobilize the whole personality to obsessive fulfillment (Hitler); the idea that the end justifies the means can encourage *deviant* behavior to achieve a fictionalized goal: astrologically this is a strong Earth Sign tendency, the Moon in Capricorn especially. The fiction that all men are created equal can discourage individual assertion: astrologically this is a strong Air Sign tendency, the Moon in Libra especially. The fiction that "I do the best I can" may lead one to bypass the practical virtue of cooperation with others in emphasizing the Self: astrologically, a strong Fire Sign tendency, the Moon in Aries especially. The fiction that "I live for my home and family" emphasizes security goals and can result in a loss of perspective in environmental challenge: astrologically, a strong Water Sign tendency, the Moon in Cancer especially.

Adler believed that the normal person could free himself from the extreme reliance upon and influence of these fictions and *face reality*, its challenges and experiences. Without this interaction with environmental reality, man defeats his creative Self; his style of life becomes self-isolating. —To a certain extent, we see the isolation of a life style within the elemental Grand Trine. But the Grand Trine emphasizes a closed circuit of *behavioral* self-sufficiency not necessarily involving a need fiction, especially when neither the Sun nor the Moon is involved (Volume IV). The Grand Trine circuit will work *to serve* the reigning need of the horoscope in a very special, routinized way. However, when the Moon itself *is* involved within the Grand Trine, the reigning need is *also* involved and the focus of life style becomes extreme, probably accompanied by a particular fictionalized finalism. For Houdini, it could have been "I am the greatest," supported by a behavioral construct "and all must know it."

Adler sought to find the goal toward which all people strive, that would give unity to personality development. The goal was something idealized, fictionalized, abstracted. For many, it is heaven, for many it is fame. Adler reached the conclusion, however, that the *unifying* goal for all is a *will to power*. He identified this will to power with the masculinity in all people, and the opposite, weakness, with femininity. He put forth an idea of *masculine protest*, a form of *overcompensation* that both sexes indulge in when they feel inadequate and inferior. The thesis of the will to power developed into *striving for superiority*. The final goal of man had three stages: to be aggressive, to be powerful, to be superior. —Every fictionalized finalism works to lift a person above a situation, to give him the feeling of superiority over those who think differently.[1]

Adler defined striving for superiority as a striving for perfect completion. —Astrologically, the person strives for a completion of his personality in terms of his reigning need. His style of life is often dictated by a goal fictionalized to help cope with reality. Adler suggested that this striving for superiority or perfection was innate. The normal person strives for goals that are primarily social, the abnormal (neurotic) person strives for egoistic or selfish goals.

Early in his career, Adler established a hypothesis of physical organ inferiority and overcompensation. He was trying to answer why people become sick in particular regions of the body: one person develops heart trouble, another nervous problems, a bad back, poor feet, etc. Astrologers have many cases of people who become sick especially in particular parts of their bodies; the tensions of frustration or the fears of inferiority appear to reside in a particular region of the body. Adler suggested that the reason for the location of a particular affliction is the basic

1. Adler was very careful to separate superiority from social distinction, but this author does not see how this is possible in practical reality since an orientation toward superiority presumes through tacit comparison that others exist not so far along the way to the same goal.

inferiority of that region. He observed that individuals will then strive to overcome this inferiority by strengthening the part through intensive study or training. Demosthenes is the classic example: he stuttered as a child and, in adult life through extreme conditioning, became a famed orator in his world. Biographies of the famous often show overcompensations of this kind: Jack Parr overcame stuttering to become a national television talker, magicians and ventriloquists have overcome shyness through public performance and illusion, athletes have overcome physical handicaps of early childhood. —The horoscope reveals the inferior part through planetary aspects and rulerships of Houses VI and XII.

In example 1, page 8, the young man's Mercury in Taurus (speech, throat) was square Pluto and, through conjunction with the Sun, took on the square from Mars, ruler of Aries on VI. The entire complex was seen within his vocal stuttering as well.

Houdini, example 2, page 12, had a basic inferiority not in his body but in his judgment. The powerful T Square Saturn-Uranus and Mars finally was his undoing but, during his life, was the reservoir of energy that his Grand Trine deployed in enormous overcompensation for this potentially threatening weakness of bad judgment. The inferior function, the weakness, was overcompensated for to the extreme, the energy converted through inspiration and discipline.

Freud's Mars was debilitating, as we have seen (example 3, page 36). The dynamic interrelationships of his horoscope found a way to forestall the difficult T

Square through the extraordinarily developed thinking function within the personality. Mars rules the mouth; Jupiter rules Sagittarius on VI and is in the T Cross with Mars and Saturn; Saturn is in Gemini (communication) and in House XII, ruled by Mercury in Taurus, the throat. Freud had enormous energy to write his theories in voluminous works, to give innumerable lectures, and to talk his way into the unconscious of his patients; and Freud died of cancer of the mouth. (This subject will be amplified in Volume IX, when illness is intensively studied astrologically.)

Adler broadened the concept of organ inferiority to include *any* feelings of inferiority. He equated inferiority with unmanliness or femininity. Then the theory came to rest in the concept of inferiority as a sense of *incompleteness* or *imperfection* in any sphere in life. He contended that inferiority feelings are not a sign of abnormality. Rather, *they are the stimulus of man's self-improvement.*

Retrogradation in Astrology is a very pertinent measure of inferiority feelings—in the sense of stimulus to self-imporvement—expecially Saturn retrograde. We know that retrogradation is a counterpoint within the scope of meaning of the particular planet. With Saturn, it would be a counterpoint within ambition. Often it corresponds to a sense of inferiority absorbed early in life, usually involving the father or the mother as the father figure: confirmation of the early Self is not received, parental endorsement is missing because a parent is out of the picture early or is not involved with the child. The young Self *creates* a deep overcompensation, a sense of individual *superiority* that helps to preserve self-esteem and forward ambition. This construct of overcompensatory superiority then protects the internal core of inferiority feelings. The personality uses the shield of superiority to protect the weak inner Self.

In interaction with the environment, the social personality with Saturn retrograde unconsciously invites exploitation by others, as if to say: "I will go along with what you say and want, because it will not really get to me inside." The role of Saturn retrograde is dramatically emphasized when, in adult life through progressions after birth (Volume VI), Saturn often is able to resume direct motion. Then, amazingly, the counterpoint falls away, ambition is freed or reapplied in singular focus, the screening process of defense is abandoned. Conversely, when the direct Saturn assumes retrograde motion during the adult life, the astrologer looks for an introduction of subtle counterpoint, the assumption of defensive, inferior feelings within the personal ambition and style of life.

In Nixon's horoscope, example 4, page 38, Saturn is retrograde in House IX, ruler of the Sun-Sign Capricorn upon House V. As a schoolboy, Nixon was eager to be a football player. He talks about it still; his love for sports is well known (House V, sports; as well as IX the natural House of Sagittarius). Nixon barely made the team as a substitute and was not a very good player. This is not important in the grand scheme of his accomplishments, but it is certainly important to his personality development. He internalized an inferiority complex about himself athletically, which was surely not alleviated by his parents. But Saturn also was squared by Nixon's Moon. His need to excel within the public, uniquely, was born. The House IX position of Saturn gained ascendancy and became law, ethics and internationalism for the maturing personality. Nixon excelled in academic studies, in the Adlerian view because of overcompensation for the weak personal ambition fulfillment in early life, probably linked with sports and personal leadership. Saturn resumed direct motion when Nixon turned twenty and graduated from Whittier College to enter Duke University Law School. His ambitions finally found direct focus and developmental application.

The bullfighter example, page 72, shows Saturn retrograde in House VI. Again, there is an athletic overtone, with Saturn ruling the Sign upon the fifth cusp and squared by Mars from IX. This is the reservoir of powerful energy and threatening bad judgment that drives the matador to prove his artistic point professionally through such an extreme duality. This Saturn will remain retreograde for the rest of his life.

Jacqueline Kennedy Onassis' Saturn was retrograde in House II (money, personal worth), ruling Capricorn on III (travel, communications, thinking, brethren). Her Saturn opposed Venus in Gemini in House VIII. Saturn resumed direct motion in her 33rd through 34th year, 1962 and 1963, the year of her first husband's assassination, leaving her alone to reconstruct a new image of her significance and personal ambitions. The previous epoch of her life could be viewed as an overcompensation in the area of personal worth because of her broken marriage homelife as a young girl.

Dwight Eisenhower had a *direct* Saturn in his House VI (service, sickness) squared with Neptune and Pluto in House II. Saturn assumed *retrograde* motion in his 76th through 77th year, a time of illness, one year before he died of a heart attack, certainly with his ambitions fulfilled on the professional level (Saturn rules Capricorn upon X, with Mars in conjunction with the Mid-Heaven, trine Saturn). Perhaps death saved him from mounting feelings of uselessness (inferiority).

Inferiority feelings are extremely difficult to discern within overcompensation. Often they will manifest themselves within the House meanings of Saturn's position. Experience with synthesis and many horoscopes will bring the overcompensation function, the counterpoint function into clearer focus for the student. Saturn retrograde is an extremely important guide into any horoscope. (Note especially the defense mechanisms discussed in chapter 5).

Retrogradation of the other planets will also indicate possible feelings of inferiority: with Mercury, a counterpoint to develop the mind and senses to a better level; with Venus, a counterpoint to develop the emotions and emotional responses to a superior level; with Mars, a counterpoint to lift applied energy to a superior level by overwork, usually, by strategic retention of energy for fear that spontaneous application might be wrong; and with Jupiter retrograde, an   aloneness to as   a strength, because of a fear of inferior reception in external relationships. Often, as Adler hypothesized, retrogradation—indications of self-shielding inferiority systems—are enormous *sources of strength.* The counterpoint is *preparation for freedom* within direct motion. If direct motion does not come into the life (as often with Saturn), the personality becomes obviously keyed to the unresolved function of the retrograde planet, and overcompensation reigns. (Lyndon Johnson: Saturn retrograde in Aries in House IX, quincunx Mars-Sun-Moon-Mercury in House I.)

Adler theorized that everyone has the same goal of superiority but develops the effort to attain it in innumerable ways. Astrologically, we observe this through the retrograde planets. *—If there are no retrograde planets,* the inferior dimension may be one of the functions we studied in chapter 2 (Jung) or a group need (chapter 3) or the whole meaning of a debilitated planetary group. Example 1, page 8, is a perfect example: no retrograde planets, enormous social-communication tension, the debilitated functions contained within the stellium in House VII, "attacked" by Mars. *If the native had retrograde planets,* the counterpoint might have provided a source of contrapuntal strength for self-consolation.

For Adler, the style of the life—the interworkings of all the planetary conditions within the horoscope—becomes the compensation for the particular inferiority, the incompleteness of the personality. —This author suggests that the drive for completion, for superiority, could indeed be the ultimate fictionalized finalism: perhaps self-completion with the creative principle after death.

Two other psychologists have developed theories that are important modifiers of the Adlerian thesis. Erich Fromm (born in Frankfurt, Germany, in 1900; in the United States from 1933) suggested in his *Escape from Freedom* that man feels lonely and isolated because he becomes separated from nature and from other men.

Man gains freedom when he leaves his parents, more freedom when he leaves his school community, even more when he gains a partner in marriage, a job, a position, retirement, death. Yet, with every acquisition of freedom, there is a sense of isolation, helplessness, loneliness. The slave gains his freedom only to find himself lost in an alien world.

What is Fromm's answer to this dilemma: "Man can either unite himself with other people in the spirit of love and shared work or he can find security by submitting to authority and conforming to society. In the one case, man uses his freedom to develop a better society; in the other, he acquires a new bondage."[2] —The Nazi dictatorship *appealed* to a depressed German people because it offered them a new security—and superiority.

Fromm means that understanding personality is based upon understanding man's needs in the "conditions of his existence." The Adlerian drive for superiority, for completion, necessarily involves social interaction and

2. Calvin S. Hall and Gardner Lindzey, *Theories of Personality* (New York: John Wiley & Sons, Inc., 1957), p. 127.

certainly an accumulation of freedoms for relationship and expression.

All people, to varying degrees, are presumably aware of the dilemma of freedom. Astrologically, we can see this dimension most keenly for those with the Sun or Moon placed in Houses VIII or XII. In House VIII, the life-energy or the personality's form, the personality's needs, will be linked to deep concerns of self-preservation and development; in XII, they will be linked to large social structures or locked away in a private prison. In these House positions, freedom (change, new opportunity, challenge) is feared to the extent suggested by the aspect condition of the lights. It is difficult for the personality energy, form, and needs to be influenced within these positions. The personality can often appear *unreachable,* privately protected in VIII or institutionally (or psychically or neurotically, etc.) shielded in XII.

Any planet in House VIII or XII will gain this undertone. In example 1, page 8, we have already studied the significance of the Moon in VIII. In Houdini's horoscope (page 12), Jupiter retrograde in House VIII calls attention again to inferiority feelings, as if the organism instinctively realized that it was threatened with the results of bad judgment within opportunity and challenge, and feared an inferior reception in external relationships. All of Houdini's escapes were extremely solitary adventures, out of view, underwater, underground, behind curtains. This Jupiter trined Pluto in House III and opposed Mercury linking his mind creatively to perspectives that were indeed peculiar: the conquering of death (House VIII) and communication thereafter (III). Houdini's escape to freedom each time was still within the restraints of his reigning need.

Edgar Cayce (example 5, page 40) had the Pisces Sun in House VIII. He was bound within his genius contact with another world. He dropped out of school before highschool, was several times attacked by the news media and threatened with jail sentences . . . but always remained self-possessed, imperturbable, strangely unreachable. He prophesied while asleep.

In example 6, page 44, the systems analyst gains personal strength only through his function within large industrial organizations. It would be extremely difficult for him—this Aries (!)—to start his own business alone, because of the many introversion factors and the House XII Moon.

The neuropsychiatrist Harry Stack Sullivan (21 February 1892, Norwich, New York) saw anxiety as a product of interpersonal relations. The *self-system* acts as guardian of one's security and tends in development to become isolated from the rest of the personality. It protects the personality from criticisms and, astrologically, corroborates Fromm's thesis that we can often see most clearly through the placement of the lights in House VIII or XII. Sullivan studied the tendency of the personality to *type* others, to establish fictionalized personifications—the hard-headed businessman, the bad mother, the absent-minded professor, the dirty Hippie, the charlatan astrologer, etc.—to help cope with others in an *impersonal* way . . . perhaps to avoid the dangerous freedom of interaction and exposure of the Self.

Sullivan stated clearly that tensions are transformed by performing work. This includes not only muscular expression and the release of nervous energy but the release as well of tension in perception, memory, thinking, creating, and relating. Tension systems accumulate throughout life as the system is *educated* through experience in how to react to social interaction and needs. —Astrologically, again we look to the lights when they are positioned in VIII or XII: there is a very strong desire to cultivate the Self significantly through personal development (VIII) or through institutional or otherworldly performance (XII). Of the presidents since Franklin Roosevelt, only Truman and Kennedy can be offered as examples: both had the Sun in VIII.

With Adler, Fromm, and Sullivan, we are discussing very sensitive nuances of personality theory. These men were building upon the work done by Freud, for the most part, and relating personality development to a world that was quickly becoming extremely modern and busy. Social change brought trauma, a loss of personal security. Economic depression and war emphasized the collectivity and minimized the individual. Then, peace and prosperity brought emphasized individual identity and the responsibility of renewed self-reliance. Change and development had become synonymous with a fearful kind of tension. Now, in the fullness of modern times, against the background of exalted individual freedoms, the challenge of social goals, allegiances, responsibilities, and life plans can be bewildering. Modern astrological analysis must recognize modern social emphases. Astrology should help delineate the responsibilities of the individual freedom part within the grander social whole. The freedom can be meaningless and impotent unless related to the environmental field that includes all individuals.

In Astrology, we study the personality within the process of becoming, within the timed development of change, accompanied by the same essential tensions postulated by psychology. Management of the tensions within change becomes the challenge to the self-system's particular individual strengths and functional potentials. A drive to completion, to a fulfillment of personal freedom, must relate interpersonally with the drives of others. The individual in his own superiority is a social part and reflects the whole. Self-protection gives way to self-application and relationship. The perspective of the whole guides the strengthening of the incomplete part.

Summary

1. A style of life is created to gain self-fulfillment, seeking out experiences or creating them.

   Fictionalized finalisms are created to guide development into the future. If the finalisms overpower the personality, goals can be out of reach, frustrations can increase, and behavioral perspective is lost.

   The unifying goal is a will to power, a striving for superiority, for perfect completion of the personality.

2. Overcompensation of an inferior function is the process that works toward fulfillment. Incompletion or

3. imperfection in any sphere of life becomes the stimulus of man's self-improvement.

   Planetary aspects, rulerships, and retrogradation can show this functional inferiority, this incompleteness. A

4. counterpoint within retrogradation is established that may change during the life and find direct, free, or renewed application; or the counterpoint may endure throughout life to energize perpetually the process of overcompensation.

5. With development come freedoms and a departure from one style of life to adopt another. Freedoms bring self-isolation and loneliness, requiring an adjustment of the life style.

6. The challenge of change threatens the Self's completeness at any stage and introduces tension. Man must face reality and develop his Self to superior completion, overcompensating for the inferior part whose under-performance he fears.

5

The Unconscious

Sigmund Freud

Freud's theories permeate twentieth-century thought and are the background upon with other psychologists have built their own specialized theories. Freud's theories permeate astrological analysis as well.

The aim of this volume is to relate Astrology to different parts of different theories. Astrology and psychological theories relating man chiefly to social interaction measure personality through its "sunlight." Freud measured the personality's light through its shadow. —Freud's theory of the unconscious is presented last in this volume so that the meaningful dark may modify the displayed brightness in a perspective that reflects modern, positive Astrology.

The psychology of the mid-nineteenth century was based upon man's conscious mental reactions to stimuli. The reactions formed patterns and defined behavior within mental structure. The active processes were emphasized with no recognition given to passive content. —Freud attacked this level of psychology by formulating the structure of the passive, unrecognized unconscious.

Sigmund Freud was born on 6 May 1856 and died in London on 23 September 1939. He spent almost his entire life in Vienna.

According to Freud, the personality is composed of three main elements: the *id,* the *superego,* and the *ego.* Each element has its own intrinsic properties, yet the interaction among them is total. Freud postulated that the id was the primal system of the personality: the reservoir of psychic energy, everything that was inherited and that furnishes the power for the other two systems. The id cannot tolerate tension. The individual desires demand gratification through the other two systems. Reduction of tension within the id was the basis of Freud's *pleasure principle*: man unconsciously seeks the pleasure of tension reduction to avoid the pain of tension increase. Man does this through reflex actions like blinking, sneezing, coughing, and fleeing danger that reduce tension immediately—and through a primary process that Freud described as *wish-fulfillment,* the only reality the id knows. Dreams and hallucinatory experiences are the projection of id reality to reduce tension, increase pleasure, and fulfill needs.

The superego is the middle stage, the censor of the id before full reality expression is achieved through the ego. A restrictive function internalized through parents, authorities, and society during development, it is the conscience, the moral value system of the personality that makes adjustments to the needs of the id so that tension *can* be released through a bona fide *reality principle,* the secondary process.

The ego operates through the secondary process, receiving id energy that has been adjusted by the superego and presenting it for gratification in reality. The ego has control over the cognitive and intellectual functions of the personality, the dimensions that had been studied thoroughly before Freud's time. The ego controls the outlet to action, selecting and integrating what can be presented to reality for gratification.

The id is the whole-form energy of the personality. It is unconscious, unknown to the conscious Self. The unconscious is a field of nonawareness that permeates the personality.

Astrologically, the id energy would permeate every symbol, every aspect, every experience. In a very debilitated horoscope—where the superego has not been constructed well or performs poorly, and socially disruptive behavior emerges—the astrologer adopts a level of interpretation that explores more of the id than of the freely expressive ego. Often in these cases, the trans-Saturnian planets—Uranus, Neptune, and Pluto—will gain special prominence within individual behavior. These planets would be seen motivationally, more than is usual. Additionally, House VIII and Scorpio, House XII and Pisces, and to a certain extent, House IV and Cancer—the Water Signs and the Houses natural to them—are especially sensitive to registration of id energies astrologically. —But it is essential to remember, in the Freudian scheme seen astrologically, that *every planet, aspect, House is describing id potential*. It is the synthesis of the horoscope that determines the balance between unconscious tensions and reality fulfillment.

Example 9: Charles Manson
November 12, 1934; 4:40 PM, EST
Cincinnati, OH

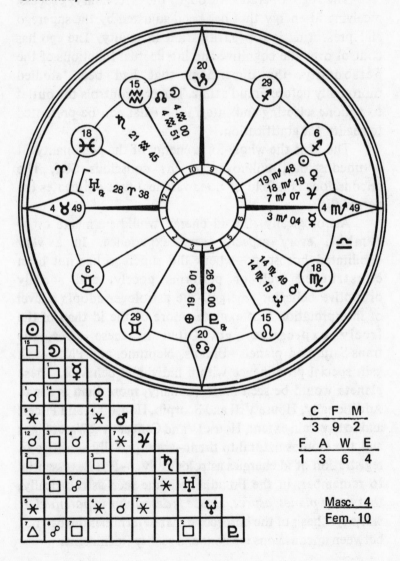

C F M
3 9 2

F A W E
1 3 6 4

Masc. 4
Fem. 10

Charles Manson's horoscope, example 9, page 98, analyzed in Volume IV and presented here once more, shows a crucial pathology: Manson's id would be seen through *Uranus* at the Ascendant, intercepted in House XII, square Pluto in Cancer in House IV, square the Moon in X, opposed Mercury in Scorpio. This Grand Cross (with the Moon and Mercury over the sign-lines) is a rigid construct that speaks of id energy. Neptune is in exact conjunction with Mars in House V. The retrogradation of Uranus and Pluto contributes to the id counterpoint as well.

Through drugs (Neptune-Mars), Manson gained the vision (primary process) of his deranged motivation and the dangerous application of Self to fulfill the wishes for superiority, love, and sex (Mars, House V). He sought this first through the entertainment industry, was rebuffed, and turned to Messianic delusion to project himself upon society uniquely. This reigning need (Moon in Aquarius, conjunct the north node) overwhelmed his superego function and discharged id energies into reality with no modification.

Specifically, within any horoscope, Saturn is the planet representing the superego functions, the internalization of society's disciplines and values, the selector of self-expression, the architect of self-ambition. Through the transit of Saturn within the lifetime (Volume VII), the restrictions, the laws, the do's and don't's of the personality are internalized and structured. In Manson's horoscope, Saturn is square the Sun (ego) in Scorpio and square Venus (emotions, sociability), also in Scorpio. The superego is under developmental tension, surely related to the father figure (Saturn) in Manson's life. We know that there would be a strong requirement for love (Saturn in House XI) that was probably unfulfilled emotionally through his father. —Manson was born illegitimate and, with his mother, was abandoned by his father.

In Volume IV we studied the significance of the Moon conjunct its own nodal axis (possible pathology with reference to the mother). In Manson's case, which has shown abnormality in life performance, we know that the law of naturalness will order components to a negative (abnormal) level within the horoscope. We must always remember that the Self reacts totally in its parts at a singularly established level except in cases of extreme duality. Part of Manson's horoscope would not be noble and another part murderous. There are no indications of classic duality; only Mars and Neptune are in Mutable Signs and there are no planets in Gemini or Pisces. Indeed, Manson's drug world was a departure from reality, into another world and value system, but the application significance of Mars brought the other world, the id, *back to* the ego reality world, the unconscious level. Following the aspects made by each planet, it is clear that each planetary function within the horoscope is indeed tied somehow to the Grand Cross (family, the unconscious) and/or to the Mars-Neptune conjunction (specific id reference, drugs). The developmental tension within the id was too much for the superego, weakened by family trauma and drugs, and the tension gained access to ego reality.

That Saturn was in Aquarius—a social Sign—also increases the importance of the ineffective superego: the idiosyncratic behavior, instead of being censored by society, was projected to the people, to society, following the reigning need established by the Moon, also in Aquarius.

Freud postulated that *instincts* are the sole energy sources for man's behavior. Instincts motivate behavior. The whole of personality works to serve them. Freud concentrated his research upon the very early years of a person's life when nourishment and sex differentiation dominate personality development. Pathology—frustration—at an early stage conditioned adult behavior. Through psychoanalysis, Freud sought to bring to the conscious a crisis established during the early stages of development to explain the infantile cause of adult behavior. Dreams (visions) serve the adult as a primary process of wish-fulfillment and are links between the unconscious and the conscious. It is very easy to infer the pathology suffered by Manson at an early age and understand the distorted echo within his behavior at an adult stage.

When we talk about vision, creativity, or inspiration, we seem to be referring to some kind of conscious interchange between the id and the ego. For an artist, this appears to be a prime requisite. The artist's discipline of painting or sculpture technique would be a superego process, the giving of acceptable form to unconscious content. As society's own restrictions have relaxed in so many areas during the 1960s and '70s, individual superegos gain a relaxation as well. The instincts that emerge, that gain greater ego presentation—in the arts, entertainment, personal image, behavior, etc.—are sexual in orientation, have high id content in the Freudian view. (Note that Neptune was in Scorpio from 1956 through 1971.) Individuals with superegos already strongly developed feel a pressure, a tension to relax, to be freer within the society around them. The guilt trauma can be great within the contrast of change. The tension is keen. (See especially example 23, Volume IV; also note the reactions of returning prisoners of war: value systems have changed during their personal confinement.)

In example 5, page 40, Edgar Cayce certainly was in contact at a very high level with the id, the unconscious, which was disciplined by his extremely religious nature (superego) and dedicated to serving humanity. House VIII, Pisces, XII, Cancer, and IV, Scorpio are accentuated by planetary positions and rulerships. Pluto is square Uranus and so is the Moon. The Moon and Neptune are in conjunction. Saturn in Pisces is in an "idealism" conjunction with Mercury and Venus, sextile the Moon and Mars. The horoscope synthesizes itself beautifully, serenely around the genius development of the unconscious and its administration (Jupiter and Mars in Capricorn, trine the Moon and Neptune) through the structure of the high-minded personality.

Freud suggested a polarization of instincts between *life instincts* and *death instincts.* The former are for survival and racial propagation, nourishment and sex. These instincts are within a hypothetical structure called the *libido.* It is within the libido that Freud concentrated upon the many subdivisions of the sex need (creativity) serving the life instinct.

Freud placed the death instincts deep in the unconscious and saw their definite existence in the reality that all men do die. In *Beyond the Pleasure Principle* he formulated the now famous idea that "the goal of all life is death." He wrote that life was a circuitous way to achieving the inorganic balance of death, a freedom from tension of development. From the death instincts was derived the aggressive drive, wherein aggressiveness directed toward self-destruction was turned outward against *substitute* objects. The life and death instincts fuse in normal life: man kills animals to gain food for his own system; love (sex) can neutralize hate (death).

This hypothesis is not at all far removed from everyday behavior or personality expression. How many times does one hear death-wishes about the Self or others during periods of frustration: "I was so embarrassed, I wanted to die" . . . or "drop dead!" . . . or "I will give my life for you." Of course, these references are hyperbole, overexaggeration. They are fictionalized releases of id tension; the death instinct gains the impulse of aggression and is released into reality. It occurs often enough, necessarily (!), that the wish has gained social acceptance and understanding. Indeed, the wish to die for one's country . . . or the order to do so, has become virtue in our society.

In example 8, page 72, one could see the dimension of the death-wish, turned into aggression, against the symbolic object of the bull, absorbed within social tradition and quasi-religious pageantry. Again, the Houses, Signs, and planets that can be associated most with the unconscious id are involved: Scorpio is on IV, the end of life as well as new beginnings. It is ruled by Pluto in Cancer, in close square with Uranus in House VIII, which has Pisces on the cusp. Jupiter is the ruler of Sagittarius, intercepted in IV, and co-ruler of Pisces on VIII. Jupiter is in House XII, in opposition with the Moon. Neptune is ruler of Pisces on VIII and is square the Sun in Gemini. The matador-artist's personality has a powerful dualism as we have seen, linked to his aesthetic vision and the fixed reservoir of energy of the T Square. —The superego has been developed with ease: Saturn in exact trine with the Sun (ego), though not without the duality counterpoint (retrogradation) and spur to resolution (square with Mars). The matador discharges the energy of the death-wish (in Freudian terms) through the killing of the bull. The rationale is the aesthetic acceptance by the public and the aesthetic discipline that he as artist values. Pluto with Venus in XI, the House of wishes and goals, blends the death instinct with the social-artistic instincts through the conjunction and other aspects and rulership references. The native's needs are powerful: the American went all the way to Spain, broke into a closed profession, to gain unique release and fulfillment.

It is interesting to note the overtones of martyrdom (with regard to tension, to stimulus, to values) often seen through the Sign Pisces. Pisces is the Mutable, changeable member of the unconscious family of Signs. Through planetary functions within the Sign Pisces, there always seems present the giving up of, or the giving in to some vital portion of the Self's functions. The martyr need is closely related to the death instinct, the adaptation need within the organism, in the Freudian view, to avoid tension by acquiescence. —Cayce gave his Self up to other powers, to live through life for his place in heaven after death. —The sacrifice of Jesus ended the Age of Pisces.

Every personality theory deals with the management of tension. For Freud, the environment with which a person interacts contains regions of danger and insecurity. The environment can threaten as well as reward through the satisfaction of needs. Freud saw that *anxiety* floods the ego when it is overwhelmed by tension from the environment and excessive need demand from the psyche. —Astrologically, any square aspect (and often the opposition) will indicate developmental tension. Tension can be active aggression or passive anxiety. Specifically, we look to Mercury and its relationship with Mars and Uranus; to Uranus and Mars and their relationship with each other or with the Sun and Moon.

In *Inhibitions, Symptoms, and Anxiety* Freud recognized three types of anxiety: *reality anxiety* is the fear of actual dangers in the physical world; *neurotic anxiety* is the fear that the instincts will get out of control, break through the superego, and bring punishment from the environment; *moral anxiety* is the fear of conscience, feelings of guilt from a well-formed superego. He showed anxiety as a behavioral drive in itself. The person will flee from the environment, censor the dangerous instinct, or obey the conscience. —Freud saw the birth trauma (the birth moment) as the key focus of anxiety in man.

The ego works to resolve anxiety through three major functions: by *identification* the person takes over the personality features of another person and incorporates them into his own personality. He reduces tension by modeling himself after someone not under tension, by imitation of someone who has conquered the anxiety in question. By *displacement* a substitute is found upon which to release tension. In frustration, a person will attack a thing or person not at all connected with the source of anxiety. Christ crucified by man, having died for men's sins, is the ultimate displacement. By *sublimation,* instinctual tensions are raised to a higher social level of achievement, channeling the energy into more noble pursuits.

Many of Freud's psychoanalytical observations reflect behavioral attitudes shared by all men at all levels. These attitudes permeate personality reactions. They are more observable in personal dialogue between astrologer and client than they are within the actual horoscope. But one can suggest that the Fire and Air Signs (and planets within them and ruling them) will work to remove anxiety more swiftly than the other Signs, perhaps more by identification. The Water Signs (and planets within them and ruling them) would work to remove anxiety more by sublimation. The Earth Signs (and planets within them and ruling them) would work to remove anxiety more by displacement. —These anxiety-removing processes are rarely completely satisfactory, mainly because they are unrealistic and incomplete. The Mutable Sign in any family will be most flexible in trying different methods, but there will always be residual tension.

When the ego is under excessive tension or accumulated residual tension, Freud saw that the ego adopted certain *defense mechanisms. Repression* occurs when the object source of the tension is put out of mind, out of consciousness. This tendency astrologically would be seen in a particular northern hemisphere emphasis. *Projection* occurs when the source of internal anxiety is identified with an external force, an objective fear, that is more easily avoided. Astrologically, this tendency would be seen in a particular southern hemisphere emphasis. *Reaction formation* is the defense measure that displaces the anxiety complex by the *opposite* complex, characterized by extravagance, showiness, or compulsiveness in the personality. Astrologically, any section of the horoscope that is extremely over emphasized *in actual behavior* may be a defense of the anxiety-ridden opposite section. For example: a tremendous stress in the ego portion, the eastern hemisphere, seen in eccentric behavior, might be an overcompensating defense against the fear of relationships, of marriage. *Fixation* and *regression* occur when the tension of the present drives the personality back to an earlier stage of development when tensions were minimal or under control. Astrologically, this is often remarkably revealed in dialogue when opportunity (change, tension) is at hand for the client, but the person prefers to live in the memory of a past period and to preserve the status quo as it was lived, as if thinking, "Why can't things be the way they were?"

Freud's works include mainly case studies of pathological people. The astrologer in normal practice meets such extreme cases only rarely if ever at all. In studying the possible applications of Freud's theories to Astrology, one must bear in mind that *all people have the potential to behave according to his hypotheses,* and that *most people have made stabilizing adjustments.* —Yet, when a person has his horoscope read, he is invariably at a point of tension. The observations of psychological theorists can be of invaluable help in reading the horoscope and being of service.

For example, in example 6, page 44, the native was troubled about the new direction his professional future would offer him. Certain progressions and transits indicated that such a change was at hand. The professional concerns were explored fully and, although this astrologer knew there was more for the client to say, the client resisted. The mechanism of repression was defending the Aries ego in its introversion (chapter 2). The professional dimensions were studied with reference to the partnership House VII that was under strong transit accentuation. The native *was* able to talk about his fears that he could not maintain his high status within the company alone, his immediate superior and friend, his "partner," with whom he identified in work operations, having just left the company and gone to another country. —The native was *not* able to talk about the other meanings of House VII, the spouse; the native denied any anxiety about his wife. It was repressed but did rise to the surface a few months later when the tension became too great. A further analysis was made, and the problems were resolved. The defenses had been removed. Tension had remained between the two consultations since part of the House VII significances had remained repressed. When released to the conscious, House VII affairs became accessible for resolution.

Nixon's horoscope, example 4, page 38, suggests both projection and reaction formation: as a patriotic politician, the "enemy" is the other party or the foreign powers that threaten to undermine the national system. Nixon was a young congressman, still with residual inferiority feelings (chapter 4) in 1948. Nixon's ambition was arch and earned him the reputation of a ruthless political strategist that endures today. Nixon made his mark by leading that era's over-reaction against communists, specifically against Alger Hiss. In Freudian dynamics, this would have been a projection by Nixon, with the displacement upon Hiss, of his own insecurity tension about performance as a congressman and lawyer, resulting in a reaction formation of overzealous patriotic achievement. Freud would certainly have gone on to analyze Alger Hiss' appropriateness as a target, i.e., his name Hiss fulfilling the psychodrama of good against evil.

Fixation and regression could be behind much of Edgar Cayce's inability to complete school or develop professionally. He progressed little past his boyhood when visions told him of his power to help others and gave him illumination. Cayce's horoscope shows his passively residing at a stage without tense development. The focus was found early in life, and the rest of the life lost a scheme of development within time. What tensions there may have been were sublimated to a lofty ideal. —The trance, the sleeping process that produced his prophecies and healing power, could be viewed as a primary process of contact with the id, a dream fulfillment; as a Freudian regression defense against a challenging, changing world; and a fixation upon a time of inspiration and beauty in the past . . . in another dimension.

It must be repeated that, most often, the nuances of defense mechanisms are revealed best in personal dialogue between astrologer and client. This topic is developed further in Volume X, *Astrological Counsel.* Freud's psychoanalytic technique of *free association* is emphasized there as well.

In conclusion, it is clear that the function of the superego is dominant in personality behavior. Saturn stands at the doorway between id endowment and ego expression. The Sun receives what Saturn has allowed to pass from the primal store of energy within the id. The master astrologer Dane Rudhyar, in his book *The Astrology of Personality,* first published in 1936, described the Sun as the "integrator" in personality. He saw Saturn as the *I* and the Sun power as *am.* The personality exists in the phrase *I am.*

In our inspection of Freud's theory, we suggest a change in this symbology. We see the Sun as ego power, the light shined upon reality, the *I;* and Saturn as the integrator *am,* the selective force within the process of becoming. —Indeed, neither exists without the other.

The superego function is the key, the balancer between tension presented by the id and tension allowed expression through the ego. It is the boundary between the unconscious and the conscious, the trans-Saturnian and intra-Saturnian planets; and it is the ambition of the personality to develop to completion. The synthesis of the horoscope defines the expression of the Self within its own disciplines. —Is not the synthesis of every horoscope itself the superego that guides fulfillment of every personality?

Summary

1. The personality is composed of the id, the superego, and the ego. The id is the reservoir of all psychic energy. The energy is censored by the superego and admitted to the ego for fulfillment in reality. The values of the superego are absorbed through parents, teachers, and society during development. Astrologically, we see the superego best through Saturn s Sign ana House position, its aspects, and transits during life.

2. The primary process is wish-fulfillment, a dream or hallucinatory reality that reduces tension with the id. The secondary process is the whole reality of the ego.

3. The unconscious is most specifically seen through the trans-Saturnian planets, the Signs of the Water Family, and Houses VIII, XII, and IV.

4. Freud postulated that instincts are the sole energy sources for man's behavior. Instincts are polarized between life instincts (survival and propagation) and death instincts. The life instincts function within a structure called the *libido*. The death instincts are hidden within the unconscious and give rise to the aggressive drive, wherein aggressiveness directed toward self-destruction is turned outward against substitute objects.

5. Anxiety floods the ego when it is overwhelmed by tension from the environment and excessive need demand from the psyche. There are three types of anxiety: reality, neurotic, and moral.

6. The ego works to resolve anxiety through three major functions; identification (more frequently by Fire and

Air Signs), displacement (Earth Signs), and sublimation (Water Signs). Excessive anxiety gives rise to defense mechanisms: repression (northern hemisphere), projection (southern hemisphere), reaction formation (the opposite developed), fixation and regression (seen best through dialogue analysis).

6

Psychological Concepts
Viewed Astrologically

The lexicon that follows includes many psychological terms and personality traits translated into astrological terms to guide further thoughts, observation, and refinement by the student.

accident prone. Accidents are chance happenings originating in the personal, social, national, or natural environment—or happenings invited by rash, heated, forceful, or frustrated projection of the personality. They are reliably suggested by Mars square the Sun, especially when the Sun is in a Fire Sign and/or placed in Houses III, IX, or I. Mars or Uranus in conjunction or opposition with the Sun; or Uranus square the Sun suggests heightened temperament that can also lead to accident, especially at times of anger. (This is a large subject that will be developed in Volume VII.)

aggression. Aggression is applied energy, seen astrologically through Mars; it is the energy stimulus for growth, development, progress. Maslow stated that when

115

frustration is removed, aggression disappears (page 63). Freud saw aggression as the death instinct turned outwards (pp.102-103.) The aspect condition of Mars will suggest the mode, intensity, and experiential focus of aggression. Additionally, Cardinal Signs afford aggression more readily than Fixed or Mutable Signs; a southern or western hemisphere emphasis affords easier outlet.

alcoholism. Alcoholism is a defense-escape mechanism used to reduce tension or dull the awareness of tension. It is usually seen through afflictions among planets within the Water Signs, especially the Moon debilitated in Scorpio, a debilitated Pisces Ascendant, often with a poorly conditioned Neptune in House I and/or square, trine, or conjunct the Sun.

altruism. Altruism is an extreme regard for and devotion to others, the opposite of selfishness; it is indicated by a conspicuous western hemisphere orientation and positive aspects to bodies in House VII; and it is usually accompanied by a Venus-Mercury conjunction, most pronounced in Cancer, Pisces, or Gemini. Saturn and Jupiter are very important as well when positioned in Libra or Sagittarius (Saturn), Sagittarius or Aquarius (Jupiter).

ambition. Ambition is the reality focus of the personality's need; the public frame of self-esteem; the professional extension of the Self, as seen through Saturn's Sign and House position. (See also *drive* and *self-esteem.*)

ambivalence. Ambivalence refers to simultaneous attraction to and repulsion from an object, idea, or person; simultaneous but unintegrated positive and negative feelings. Ambivalence can be suggested when the Moon makes a square and a trine to two different planets, which in turn are related to each other by mutual reception or are both prominent in position; or when the Moon is in Gemini or Pisces and under strong positive and negative tension. (See example 3, page 36.)

anxiety. Anxiety is tension and is indicated by square and opposition aspects, or conjunctions of Uranus and the Sun or Mercury. Nervous anxiety is suggested by Uranus square, opposed, or conjunct Mercury, especially in Mutable Signs. Anxiety is essential developmental tension for personality fulfillment. Synthesis of configurations will determine the anxiety outlet. The T Square is a reservoir of energy that becomes debilitatingly anxious without outlet. Anxiety suggests frustration. Frustration stimulates aggression.

athletic. Athletic interests are indicated by a strong V and/or IX or a prominence of Leo and Sagittarius; Mars and Jupiter suggest ability; the Sun, ability and success; and Pluto, the spectator role.

beauty. Beauty in appearance is suggested by Libra on the Ascendant or Venus well-aspected and rising.

camouflage. Neptune within any House suggests

camouflage, unusualness, repression, or substitution pertaining to the House meanings in the quality suggested by the Sign and the aspects received. Something is not as it seems. In the Ascendant Neptune indicates dream life or sensitive organism.

carefulness. Attention to detail is a Mercury function at its best in the Earth Signs, at its worst (carelessness) in Gemini, Saggittarius, or Aries, or in square, opposition, or conjunction with Neptune or Pluto. Carefulness is often accompanied by caution: Capricorn, Taurus, Scorpio.

communication. Communication is a Mercury function that gains application support from Mars. Mercury's Sign suggests the nature of the communication skill; the House of Mercury suggests the best source or medium of communication. Additionally, Houses III and IX are important; also, the Signs Gemini, Leo, Sagittarius and their articulation within synthesis.

compensation. Through growth and experience, as suggested by Adler and Jung, the personality discovers and develops an inferior function to eliminate disadvantage. Through astrological progressions, new patterns form in developmental compensation to reorganize strengths and weaknesses in the personality.

compulsion. A highly delineated focus of motivation and applied energy, compulsion is strongest in self-contained aspect patterns like the Grand Trine, the

Grand Cross, and the T Cross, especially when they involve the Moon and Mars. Fixed Sign emphasis shows maximum compulsive fixation to serve the reigning need.

conservatism. A function of Saturn, especially in conjunction with the Sun or Moon, conservatism through a sense of responsibility is suggested by Saturn opposing the Sun or by Saturn rising, especially in Sagittarius, Capricorn, or Libra. Retrogradation may be subsidiary measurement suggesting caution or counterpoint within conservatism. A New-Moon birth(within three degrees orb) suggests listlessness rather than conservatism. Conservatism is mainly an Earth Sign characteristic.

cooperative. Cooperativeness is a Mutable Sign characteristic, especially when Mutable Signs occupy the angles of the horoscope.

creativity. Each Sign has its own special nature that—when developed aesthetically or artistically through Venus or Neptune, ingeniously through Uranus, conservatively through Saturn, or publicly through Pluto—becomes especially creative. Jupiter expands creativity through opportunity and enthusiasm. Mars applies creativity.

critical nature. A critical nature is indicated especially by the Sign Virgo, also Gemini, but with less value judgment; it is usually accompanied by delay and indications of conservatism.

depression. Psychologically, depression suggests a person caught in a dilemma. Anxiety is kept inside. A horoscope with Saturn rising, especially retrograde, and/or Mars in a Water Sign, especially retrograde, open the personality to depression. The Moon in House I inclines to moodiness and temperament fluctuation. Depression suggests the inability to make a choice (afflictions in Gemini) and to apply energy to forward ambition.

destructiveness. Strong square complexes from Mars and/or Uranus, especially between two hemispheres, indicate destructiveness. If synthesized positively through supportive aspects involving Pluto, destructiveness becomes reform; aggression finds positive outlet through a focused goal or through sublimation.

detachment. Detachment is an unwillingness to open the personality to change or adjustment and a reliance upon other dimensions to satisfy needs and release tensions. Neptune rising accentuates the value of dreams. Mercury opposed Neptune suggests daydreaming. Stubborn, inaccessible detachment is suggested through Fixed Sign constructs. An eastern hemisphere emphasis suggests a difficutlty in fulfilling relationships; as do Neptune or Pluto conjunct the Sun (often accompanied by pronounced retrogradation) and an absence of oppositions.
—The consideration of horoscope level is important: detachment can aid lift to higher realms of awareness.

dissociated complex. A dissociated complex is a group of energies isolated in extreme focus (see example 1, page 8, House VII). Boundaries around the group become fortified against permeation, especially within Fixed Signs. The group commands the whole of the personality.

dominance. Dominance is indicated by an overemphasis of the Cardinal Signs with a highly accentuated and/or elevated Saturn; by the Moon in Leo; or by Mars or Saturn square the Sun in Cardinal Signs.

dreams. High dream activity is seen through Neptune, expecially when placed in House I or X. If Neptune is unaspected, a dreamlike detachment manifests in the personality. If Neptune is well integrated within the synthesis, creativity from dream content increases. Neptune is the key planet for access to the id and the primary dream process.

drive. Drive is a synonym for motivation or need press. Personal drive goals will evolve out of the Sign and House positions of the Moon; the drive energy will be highest when Saturn or Mars squares, opposes, or conjoins the lights. Nervous drives will form within aspects among Mercury, Uranus, and Mars.

duality. More than one profession, strong parallel development of a hobby or avocation, or diversified interests are most reliably seen through the Signs Gemini and Pisces when one occupies the Mid-Heaven; additionally, when any Sign is intercepted in House X or when Gemini especially is powerfully emphasized anywhere in the horoscope.

eccentricity. Highly unusual behavior is seen through the planet Uranus, especially when placed in House I and/or square the Sun or Moon. Additionally, Uranus in the Mid-Heaven or in dynamically configurated relationship with Mercury, or emphasis on the Signs Gemini, Sagittarius, and Aquarius, indicate eccentricity.

egocentrism. Egocentrism is suggested by a highly pronounced emphasis of the eastern hemisphere, or by Mars debilitated and rising.

energy. The condition of Mars; vitality is suggested by any aspect between Mars and the Sun or Moon.

enthusiasm. Enthusiasm is a function of Jupiter, its aspects and House-Sign condition. A retrograde Jupiter does not necessarily mean withdrawn or diminution of enthusiasm; rather, a counterpoint of aloneness and profit therefrom may be introduced, which may be confining perhaps if placed in House XII or VIII.

eroticism. When Neptune is in House V and squares the Sun, Moon, Venus, or Mercury, especially prominently involving the Sign Scorpio or Pisces, the awareness of the aesthetic dimensions of sex will be important within the personality. This awareness is also indicated by the Moon in Scorpio or Scorpio on the Ascendant, and by Houses VIII, XI, and XII. Eroticism is heightened by Aquarius or Libra   rising; diminished by Virgo, Capricorn, or Gemini rising.

extravagance. Extravagance is suggested by a square between Jupiter and the Sun or Moon when Saturn is *not* prominently involved with the lights, Venus, Jupiter, or Mercury. The prominence of Leo is also often involved.

extraversion. Southern or western hemisphere emphasis, with an absence of or minimal retrogradation, indicates extraversion. Fire and Air Signs will be prominent. (See chapter 2.)

fantasy. Active imagination is suggested by Neptune prominently aspected with Mercury, the Sun, or Moon and by Houses V, VIII, III, and I. See also *dreams*.

fear. Fear is a reaction to whatever threatens the need fulfillment construct of the personality; it is suggested by the nature and experience meanings of any planets in opposition or square to the Moon or Saturn; by the planets within and ruling House XII; and by the planets afflicting the Sun.

fixation. See *dissociated complex* and *regression*.

flight into illness. A Freudian term describing the

advantage gained by the ego when the personality escapes into illness to avoid a certain fear or tension, flight into illness is suggested in the horoscope by fear significators linked through tenancy or rulership with House VI, especially with Neptune placed in VI or in conjunction or square the Moon, Sun, or ruler of VI or XII.

focus. Focus is a coming together of energies in specific meaning, seen chiefly through opposition, square, and conjunction (in order). A horoscope with no opposition or clear square is a horoscope without clear focus for energy application to fulfill the personality. Conjunctions require additional aspects for best application.

forgetfulness. Freud referred to slips of the tongue and pen and to misplacement of things as phenomena of the unconscious, often suggesting subconscious feelings and intent. In the horoscope, an afflicted Mercury, expecially in a Mutable Sign, will suggest forgetfulness (if Saturn is not involved). When Neptune is also involved, a contact with the unconscious can be suspected in the Freudian sense.

Generosity. Generosity is indicated by planets in Houses II and XI usually forming squares. There would be reasonable prudence, pressing mania, or negative outcome with regard to loaning money to friends, depending upon other related aspects. When the planets within or the rulers of Houses II and XI form *trines* (due to interception) and especially if Mutable Signs are involved and Houses VII and VIII are positive, the trait of generosity will manifest itself strongly within the personality.

Each Sign must have certain needs met before generosity can be expressed: Aries, ego recognition; Taurus, structure secured and highly valued; Gemini, interest excited; Cancer, security safeguarded; Leo, importance recognized; Virgo, details clarified; Libra, popularity assured; Scorpio, deeper significances explored; Sagittarius, opinions shared; Capricorn, dignity recognized; Aquarius, innovativeness promised; Pisces, helpfulness emphasized.

Generosity presumes a measure of enthusiasm, making Jupiter's condition within the horoscope relevant.

guilt. A manifestation of the superego (Saturn) and a reaction to ambivalence in the decision-making process, guilt appears when there is tension between the id and ego. The inclination to guilt is suggested through opposition of any planet with Saturn, especially in Mutable Signs; and through Saturn related to the Moon in a double-bodied Sign and/or placed in House VIII or XII, or in aspect with the rulers of VII or XII.

habits. Repetitious acts support the fulfillment of needs. The Moon rules the reigning need and Saturn establishes routine. The tendencies of the Sun-Sign are formalized by Saturn and expressed through the Moon. The Moon in Fixed Signs tends to stronger habit formation. Careless habits often involve an afflicted Venus in Aries and Mutable Signs on the angles. A square from Jupiter to the lights will suggest expensive habits. The Sign Taurus indicates greatest habituation.

healthiness. Psychological health is seen through aspects to the Sun, Moon, ruler of VI, and the planets in VI. The personality may be very healthy but *not* energetic, recuperatively vital. The personality may be energetic and vital but not healthy. (See *energy, vitality* and Volume IX.)

hedonism. A dedication to the pleasure principle, to living for pleasure, hedonism is suggested within the relationship between Houses V and VII, usually a sextile, is a square, involving Neptune or Pluto; especially with the Signs Scorpio, Capricorn, Libra, or Cancer. (See *eroticism, sexulaity.*)

hostility. Sun, Moon, Jupiter, and Venus weakened; Scorpio accented with debilitating aspects involving Mars, Uranus, and Saturn—these indicate hostility. The target of hostility will be shown by the focus of House positions within synthesis. Additionally, the tendency is present when Scorpio is rising and Mars squares, opposes, or conjoins Mercury.

humor. Humor is an acute perception and articulation gained through a well-placed and well-positioned Mercury; a positive House V and/or III; or the Moon in Leo in House III. Saturn is *not* in I or VII.

idealism. Psychologically, idealism is an attempted solution of conflict through the creation of an idealized image. The personality substitutes another's power and superiority, another's wholeness, to give the Self a sense of safety (often illusory). (See Freud, *identification,* page 101.) Astrologically, idealism is indicated by close conjunction between Mercury and Venus, often involving the Sun as well. The Fire and Air Signs tend to reflect idealistic identification more than the other Sign families. When the Water Signs are involved, the idealization is more spiritual in nature; with the Earth Signs, the idealization is more practical.

indecision. Indecision is a difficulty reflected in Gemini because of the swiftness of the mind and its special flexibility and restlessness; in Pisces because of the dependency upon emotional stimulus to arouse reaction; and in Virgo because of the delay for all details to be perfect, for opportunity and motivation to present themselves. —Mars in Gemini scatters the energy of self-application; Mars in Cancer or Pisces dilutes it.

inferiority feelings. Inferiority feelings, often accompanied by an apologetic attitude, is indicated by a prominent Saturn in Houses I, XII, V, or VIII, in Aries, Cancer, or Pisces especially; when the Sun or Moon is afflicted as well, the trait of inferiority is pronounced. It is also indicated by the Moon square or opposed Venus or by pronounced retrogradation. (See Adler, pages 82-88; Jung, page 32; see *introversion.*)

inhibitions. Inhibitions are a Saturn function, especially when it is prominently placed in the Ascendant and/or opposed, square, or conjunct the Sun or Moon. They are also indicated by an emphasis of the northern hemisphere and pronounced retrogradation.

intellect. Intellect, the power to understand, organize, apply, and analyze accumulated knowledge, is suggested by strong aspects among the Moon, Mercury, and Saturn, involving the Ascendant or its ruler, *without* Mars and Neptune. —Mars and Neptune gain secondary ascendancy when the structure of intellect is firm and the House references call for energetic application and artistic vision. The Sign Aries prominent indicates incisive intellect; Taurus, structured, down-to-earth intellect; Gemini, academic; Cancer, emotional, etc. Uranus or Aquarius prominent introduces the dimension of invention or social uniqueness.

intelligence. Intelligence, the absorption and awareness of data, fleetness of mind, is suggested by a Moon with accelerated diurnal motion at birth, in excess of fourteen degrees. Additionally, a direct Mercury ahead of the Sun, i.e., in greater longitude than the Sun, indicates great curiosity. The Sign and House positions of Mercury suggest the nature of intelligence and the field to which intelligence best applies. The aspects to Mercury suggest the energy factors within intelligence. Study Houses III, IX, VI, and VIII.

introversion. Introversion is associated more with Water and Earth Signs than with Fire and Air; with an emphasized northern or eastern hemisphere and pronounced retrogradation; with Saturn rising, afflicting the lights; and with especially emphasized Houses XII,VIII, or IV. (See Jung, p. 32.)

intuition. A dimension of contact with the unconscious, intuition is seen through a prominent Neptune or Pluto, especially in strong relationship with the Moon or the Sun, emphasizing Houses XII, VII, or IV; and through retrogradation. It is associated especially with the Signs Pisces, Cancer, and Scorpio. (See Freud, page 101).

joy. Joy is suggested by the Sun, especially when rising and positively aspected with Jupiter, Venus; by Jupiter or Venus rising and positively aspected; or by the Sun position at the Mid-Heaven when there are no complications within the profession. The Sign Sagittarius is significant, especially rising or with Mars well aspected therein.

A personality that feels robbed of joy in life is often suggested by the lights in House XII by affliction from Mars, Saturn, Neptune, or Pluto, or by heavy oppositions to the Sun.

judgment. Good judgment is indicated by the Sun and/or Moon dignified at birth, in good aspect with Mercury, Saturn, or Jupiter; Sagittarius rising or on the

Mid-Heaven; Scorpio rising; or a prominent, positive Mars or Jupiter. Bad judgment is associated with Mars square Saturn; with Sun conjunct Mercury and square Mars, Jupiter, Saturn, or Uranus; and with afflictions in Libra.

leadership. Leadership is relfected in an emphasis on Cardinal Signs and Leo, and in a prominent Saturn and Mars.

limitations. Limitations are seen through the planets within or ruling House XII; Saturn in a demanding aspect configuration; and the Sign Capricorn prominent or rising.

listlessness. A New-Moon birth (within three degrees) indicates listlessness. The Sun or Mars not clearly aspected at birth; the Moon in House XII, in Pisces or Taurus and in aspect with Neptune or Pluto—these also suggest listlessness.

love. House V is associated with love given, House XI with love received. Love is further associated with the condition of Venus and, secondarily, Mars. Saturn restricts and limits as does retrogradation.

luck. Good fortune is indicated by a trine or sextile between Uranus or Jupiter and the Sun or Moon, especially involving Houses II, VII, X, and XI.

magnetism. Personal magnetism is chiefly seen through the conjunction of Mars and Neptune and, to a certain extent, of Neptune and the lights. The latter has more of the mystery dimension; the former configuration, more of electric command. Additionally, the Sign Scorpio is usually prominent. (See example 9, page 98.)

masochism. Masochism is the need for sacrifice to or subjugation by others, usually accompanying depression, introversion, and inferiority feelings. The Sign Pisces is prominent and its planets or rulers are afflicted by Saturn and/or Mars. Additionally, there is an afflicted Venus and prominence of House XII. Virgo and Capricorn are also Signs sensitive to the personality defense of masochism, especially when Mercury is debilitated and Saturn squares the Moon, Sun, or Venus. —The dimension of sex enters when Mars and Venus are related within debilitation, when Uranus is involved in the synthesis, and Houses V and IX are emphasized.

melancholy. Melancholy, a pervasive sadness, is reflected in the lights and/or Mercury severely afflicted by Saturn; Venus afflicted by Saturn; with Houses VII and XII emphasized. According to Freud, it involves a withdrawal of libido (creative aggression) from an object. The ego then is treated as the abandoned object, suffering internalized aggression.

memory. Memory is suggested by aspects between Saturn and Mercury, by a well-aspected Moon, especially involving Houses I, III, and VI, and by Virgo.

metamorphosis. A revolutionary change potential

within the personality, metamorphosis is indicated by Sun conjunct Pluto, emphasis on House IV, and dimensions of duality in the horoscope. —The transit of Pluto over the Sun, Moon, or Ascendant during life also suggest change potential. The conjunction of Saturn and Uranus in the birth horoscope indicates a collision between tradition and innovation that can lead to decisive change in personality during development.

moroseness. Moroseness, thoughts of death and uselessness, is chiefly a Capricorn trait, also indicated by Saturn in I, VIII, especially in Pisces or conjunct, square, or opposed Neptune.

motivation. Motivation is the energy stimulus to fulfill a need. High motivation is associated with any aspect between the Moon and Mars, or the square or opposition between the Moon and Saturn; low motivation, with no squares involving the Moon.

musicality. Prominent Neptune; Venus in Libra or Aquarius or prominent; the Signs Leo, Pisces, and Aquarius; House V prominent—these identify musicality.

narcissism. Narcissism is love of Self, an opposite of altruism. Freud described it as the turning of the libido in upon itself, the original state of the newborn. It is suggested by a complete eastern orientation of planets with Neptune conjunct or square the Sun, involving the ruler of the Ascendant, and by V and VII as well. A sexual emphasis is introduced through Mars and its relationship with Venus and the Sun, and involving Neptune Aand Uranus, manifesting through the inordinate practice of masturbation.

need. Need is the distillation of personality requirements for fulfillment, the motivation of behavior. The reigning need of the personality is seen through the Sign and House position of the Moon (See pages 19, 57, 64, 101-102.)

nervous system. The nervous system is reflected in aspects between Mercury and Uranus and/or Mars; a square, opposition, or conjunction between Uranus and the Sun suggests a highly geared nervous system. Also relevant are the Signs Aries, Sagittarius, Aquarius, Gemini, and Virgo. (See *drive.*)

neurosis. A demonstrable psychonervous disorder, neurosis is seen when the nervous system is involved within a dramatically set off dissociated complex.(See example 1, page 8.)

paranoia. Paranoia consists of delusions of persecution integrated with delusions of personal grandeur. It is indicated by severe aspects to planets within House VII and a prominent inclusion of Neptune; emphasis of Houses VII, VIII, and I; and a prominent Saturn synthesized through square or opposition. (See discussion of Hitler's horoscope, Volume IV.)

perception. Perception is a Mercury function, especially when that planet is in Capricorn, Virgo, Aries, or Sagittarius. Additionally, it is reflected in the Sun in Virgo, Gemini, or Capricorn placed in House III or IX. When the Sun is in Scorpio or Pisces and is in VIII or XII, perception is deepened and made more subtle.

Self-perception within the world, seeing one's Self, becomes a sense of personal perspective, severely debilitated by a square or opposition between Mercury and Pluto. (See *self-esteem.*)

practicality. An emphasis of Earth Signs in the horoscope, or a prominent Saturn, suggest practicality.

Impracticality is suggested in an absence of Earth Sign activity, i.e., neither planets in Earth Signs, nor the Ascendant nor the Mid-Heaven as well; the personality senses the lack, works nervously to make even the smallest occurrence significant, and exacts performance from others.

projection. Projection identifies internal anxiety with an external force, an objective fear, so that it can be more easily managed. It is reflected in a southern hemisphere emphasis and a tendency to Fire and Air Signs. (See page 107.)

psychosis. Psychosis is a serious mental derangement; a neurotic state developed to the point of departure from reality. See as a possible example, example 9, page 98, wherein the Grand Cross formation commands the entire horoscope and the drug dimension deliberately introduces unreality.

public orientation. Public orientation is primarily seen through a prominent Pluto, upon the Mid-Heaven or in an emphasized opposition axis; also through House VII highlighted through tenancy or rulership; a prominent Moon in X or VII, especially in a Fire Sign, Aquarius, or Libra. (See example 2, page 12; example 4, page 38.)

regression. Regression is a defense mechanism triggered when the tension of the present drives the personality back to an earlier stage of development when tensions were minimal or under control. It is revealed in dialogue, possibly corroborated through deep analysis of secondary progressions (Volume VI). (See *introversion* and also page 108.)

repression. Repression is a defense mechanism that puts the object source of tension out of mind, out of consciousness; it is a particularly northern hemisphere trait. (See page 107.)

religiousness. A highly developed religious nature is suggested by an emphasized House IX, the Signs Sagittarius, Pisces, and Scorpio, and particularly by Jupiter in Scorpio or highly elevated.

sadism. Sadism is satisfaction gained by cruelty or persecution or, more frequently, the persona of coercion, the subtle control of others. It is indicated by severely afflicted Venus, prominence of Saturn, Mars, and Pluto; the Sun and Moon in square or opposition; the Moon debilitated in Capricorn or Virgo.

satirical. An ironical, ridiculing, sarcastic nature is a trait chiefly of Scorpio, Virgo, Capricorn, or Sagittarius, when planets therein or the rulers are squared or opposed Mercury, Mars, or Saturn. It is also indicated by Cancer, in defense of a threat to security.

secretiveness. Secretiveness is reflected in the Sun or Moon in VIII or XII, the prominence of Scorpio, or Neptune and Pluto, one usually in conjunction with Mercury or the ruler of the Ascendant or House III. It is a Water or Earth Sign trait especially; and associated with northern or eastern hemispheres.

self-esteem. A vital dimension in every horoscope is the personality's own self-respect: how the person sees himself in relation to his need structure (the Moon) and its fulfillment (past record); to his goals (House XI and its ruler); his professional status (House X and its ruler); and how others see him (House VII and its ruler). Additionally, self-esteem refers to the person's *own* perception of how others see him.

The superego (Saturn) is created from the internalized expectations of others, beginning with the parents and absorbed from social authorities throughout development. Saturn's elevation within the horoscope inclines to higher self-esteem than when Saturn is below the horizon. The Moon's position in a Fire or Air Sign, especially Leo or Aquarius, suggests high self-esteem. Saturn's relationship with the Moon is the core structure. The tremendous ambitious drive that corresponds to the Moon square or opposed to Saturn suggests that the personality drives ever forward to fulfill needs despite any restriction from the environment.

Self-esteem determines significantly the level of the horoscope. A positive relationship between the Sun and Moon and a well-conditioned, well-integrated Saturn helps the rest of the horoscope to expression and development within life's work. Retrogradation tends to debilitate self-esteem and can introduce a false notion of the self-image.

Additionally, Leo or Libra rising and an emphasis of the southern hemisphere incline to high self-esteem.

sexuality. Physical passion is associated with House V, VIII, and XI, their planets and rulers, especially the Sign on the fifth cusp and its ruler; also with the condition of Mars and the placement and tenancy of Scorpio. (See *eroticism.*)

speculativeness. Speculativeness is a House V condition; when related to House II or its ruler, speculation is usually financial; when related to XI or its ruler, the speculative dimension of the personality is usually social and emphasizes the wish-fulfillment process of personality development. The speculative dimension is also indicated Mars square Jupiter.

speech. Speech is associated with Mercury; the Signs Aries, Taurus, and Gemini. Underdeveloped speech function is indicated by Mercury afflicted in Houses VI, XII, or III, also involving the Moon, Saturn, or Mars in synthesis; fluency of speech is suggested by Mercury in an angle or Aries, Libra, Capricorn. Public appeal through speech is reflected in Cancer.

stubbornness. Fixed Sign prominence, especially when Fixed Signs are upon the angles, indicates stubbornness.

suicide. Suicide usually emerges from unrealistic perceptions of the self-position, a loss of defense mechanisms, and the inward turning of the death wish finally to rid the Self of tension. When Mercury is square Pluto and Neptune is also prominent, the thoughts of suicide are usually strong in the personality; also when a debilitated Mars and a planet in House XII—or its ruler—are afflicted. (See *melancholy.*)

travel. A great inclination to travel is seen through accentuation or House IX and/or III, especially involving the Signs Sagittarius and Gemini and their rulers; also, through Gemini or Sagittarius rising. When synthesis involves the ruler of IV as well, travel will include home settlement far away from the birth area.

tyranny. A severe accentuation of leadership indices, possibly involving dimensions of paranoia, indicates tyranny; also the overpowering emphasis of Mars, Saturn, and the Cardinal Signs. (See also *leadership* and *paranoia.*)

unconscious. The processes of the id, superego, and ego are specifically seen through Houses VII, XII, and IV, the Signs of the Water Family, and the trans-Saturnian planets. (See chapter 5.)

vision. Vision is signified by Neptune utilized altruistically; it is the unconscious brought into reality through the superego function of reality disciplines. (See page 101.)

vitality. Vitality is indicated by any aspect between the lights and Mars. It is not to be confused with health. (See *health, energy.*)

wisdom. Wisdom, involving *perception, intelligence,* and *intellect,* is indicated by the development of aspect relationship between Saturn and Mercury; and by the Sun or Moon trine and, often, opposed Saturn.

A person's capacity to advise is chiefly a function of Saturn, Mercury, the Signs Capricorn, Virgo, and Scorpio, and Houses III, IX, and VIII. Any aspect between Saturn and Mercury or the prominence of both in the horoscope inclines to good advisory capacity. The introduction of Sagittarius will give a higher level of judgment. Mars will be important in the application of the advisory ability, especially when well aspected and placed in House VIII, IX, or V.

7

Toward Unity

The personality whole is the unity of its parts. Astrologically, a law of naturalness orders the parts to a specific level within the whole personality. Psychologically, the interrelation of needs, tension, and fulfillments in all parts of personality life comprises the individual unit. For the Gestalt psychologists particularly, the total integrated pattern of behavior is studied in a spatial field unity similar to the horoscope chart.

Unity is the goal assumed at birth and the product achieved through life, the final freedom from tension being reached in death, a return to unity with the creative spirit. During the process of life behavior, boundaries between parts are rearranged, new levels and arrangements are created. With every step of development, there is a tension to achieve a new or greater unity. In the process of becoming, unity is a matter of degree.

The process of psychological or astrological synthesis uncovers the *inclination to unity* and defines the tensions en route. Psychology postulates stages of development within life, and Astrology measures the development of

141

inclinations within time. Both seek to understand the reason for and the efforts of change with reference to a goal of personality completion.

Beginning with Volume VI, our study turns concentratedly to the measurement of development within time. The inclination to unity taken on through birth awareness is systematically evaluated through personal and environmental tensions toward challenges and opportunities in the lifetime. The degrees of unity are analyzed in relation to performance in past time and are projected into future time, all parts of the process of becoming. The horoscope present, the birth moment, is broadened to include moments in the future, in a manner not unlike the focus of much psychoanalytical theory upon the birth trauma. The study of development within time becomes *the analysis of an expanded present.*

The work of psychologists within the twentieth century has corroborated much of what Astrology has revealed to disciplined, knowledgeable men through millennia. The terms are different and different foci are emphasized, yet both analytical systems reflect life as it is lived within time and that time's theories. The practitioner within each science has different premises, different channels and means of analysis. Each science demands an enormous commitment of time, study, practice, and dedication. Each system seeks the same goal of understanding personality.

The psychological theories cursorily covered in this volume are only parts of the ultimate unified whole of personality knowledge. The personalities who create the theories are *themselves* theories in practice and personify the very knowledge they formalize: Freud was a Taurus (with Scorpio as polar complement) and in so many text books is called the master builder. His work was an enormous overcompensatory displacement of his own severe personal difficulties. The sublimation of his traumatic energies gave birth to a colossal personality construction theory based upon recognition of the unconscious and its primal sex energy (Scorpio) that has been invaluable to the thoughts of all men in all fields. Jung was a Leo (with Aquarius as polar complement) and conceived a personality theory that gave man a position of dignity and creative function within the flow of a collective humanity, endowed with the memory of a supreme being, the creative self that gives meaning to life.

Researchers dedicate their lives, their personalities to developing theories of behavior. Every man has a natural need to know himself. Man wants to know, to become an aware part of the whole mystery. This quest is the very core of man's need to fulfill, to complete himself.

Each theory can function only in its own wholeness. A few Freudian generalities in the hands of someone not dedicated to study, observation, practice, and service are as dangerous to personality analysis as a laser beam handled incompetently is to body tissues. Similarly, rudimentary astrological deductions and principles applied without depth and skill can disrupt the very unity to which theoretical knowledge is dedicated. —The dignity of completeness is the dimension that creates a separative boundary between different theories. Psychologists of different disciplines reject Freud for his sexual and infancy emphases. Freudians reject the different disciplines that emphasize social interaction and healthy orientation. Too many psychological theories reject Astrology without knowledge of Astrology's own dignity within its own unity.

Astrology must take the lead in creating synthesis among the parts of the personality theory whole. The field of study is broad enough to include any theory, to test it, to study it, to apply it so far as the nature of the theory allows. The astrologer himself must know his discipline well in order to relate profitably with the other analytical systems.

The Harvard psychologist Gordon Allport established three criteria for maturity, a fullness of development. He postulated an *extension of self* whereby a personality gains ideals and direction through others and their values; a *self-objectification,* including insight and humor enabling one to understand and minimize developmental tension, by seeing the part of the whole as it is seen by others; and a *unifying philosophy of life* that binds the parts together and extols the whole.

The study of personality theories should well ascribe to such mature perspective. Eclecticism should replace parochialism. A blend of theories from many sources would break through the boundaries between specialty fields. The reigning need of research would be to understand, to know, and to serve.

The maturity of a theory in many ways depends upon the development of the theory's practitioner. Each theorist must have himself as his first client. Astrologers have an enormous responsibility to research and practice in maturity, to be eclectic in order to serve our fellow-man in the best way. The opening of the mind releases developmental tensions to discovery. No reactionary defense is needed if the spirit of inquiry is well disciplined and the drive to serve is responsibly fulfilled. All the theories of personality that have accumulated through time have something to offer. The astrologer inherits the wisdom of the past and adopts the knowledge of the present. He expands his present legacy as far as knowledge will allow into a future of service, integrity, and revelation.

The scope of this volume has been to introduce several major tenets of psychological personality theory as they apply to the horoscope at this stage of the student's astrological study. Psychological theories will play a role in all the volumes that follow in this series. The student is urged to read further in the field of psychology, to begin to find his own personal style of viewing the personality en route to its fulfillment. Texts are recommended in the Appendix, and ten horoscopes of famous personalities are presented for further psychological study.

Appendix

Supplementary Reading List

Metzner, Ralph. *Maps of Consciousness.*
New York: MacMillan, 1971.

Rudhyar, Dane. *The Astrology of Personality.*
New York: Doubleday, 1970.

Fordham, Frieda. *An Introduction to Jung's
Psychology.* Penguin-Pelican Books, 1953.

Hall, Calvin S. and Gardner Lindzey. *Theories
of Personality.* New York: John Wiley & Sons,
1957.

Ouspensky, P.D. *In Search of the Miraculous.*
New York: Harcourt Brace, & World, Inc.,
1949.

Study Horoscopes

Enrico Caruso, opera singer
February 25, 1873; 12:14 PM
Naples, Italy

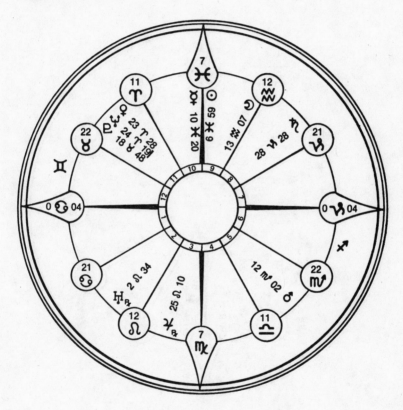

[Source: M.E. Jones]

Paul Cezanne, artist
January 19, 1839; 1:00 AM
Aix-en-Provence, France

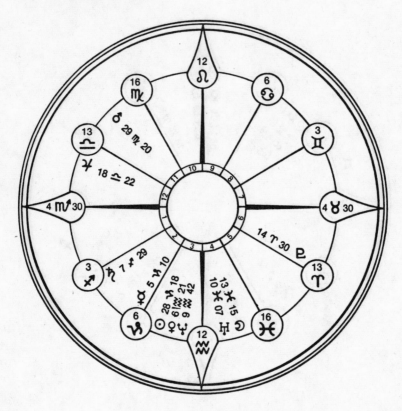

[Source: M.E. Jones]

Salvador Dali, artist
May 11, 1904; 8:45 AM
Cadaques, Gerona, Spain

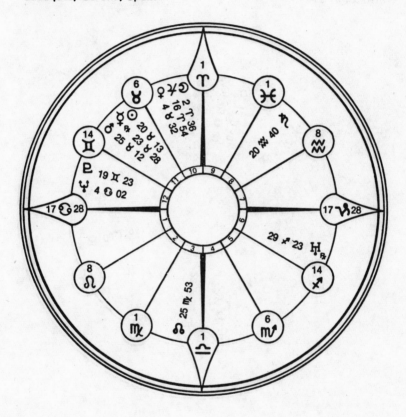

[Source: M.E. Jones]

Stephen Collins Foster, composer
July 4, 1826; 12:30 PM
Pittsburgh, PA

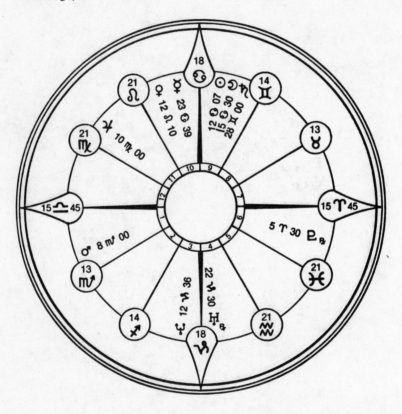

[Source: M.E. Jones]

Vincent van Gogh, artist
March 30, 1853; 11:00 AM
Groot-Zundert, Netherlands

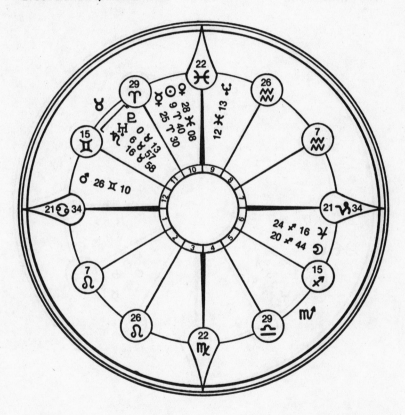

[Source: M.E. Jones]

Carl Gustav Jung, psychologist
July 26, 1875; 7:20 PM
Basel, Switzerland

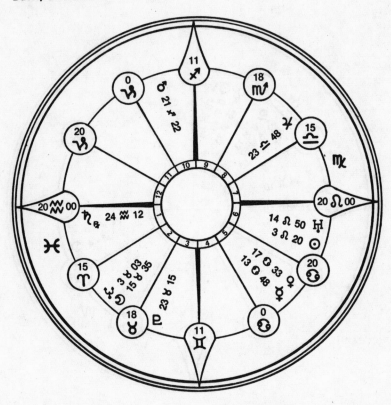

[Source: M.E. Jones]

Jeddu Krishnamurti, mystic
May 12, 1895; 12:25 AM
Madanapalle, Madras, India

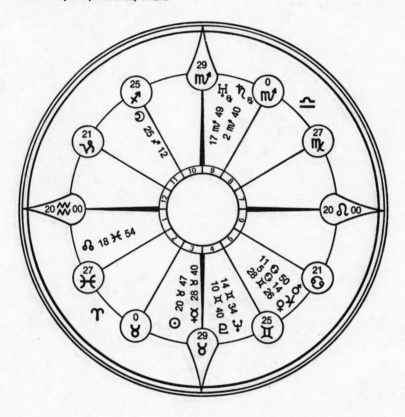

[Source: M.E. Jones]

Franz Liszt, composer-pianist
October 22, 1811; 1:16 AM
Raiding, Hungary

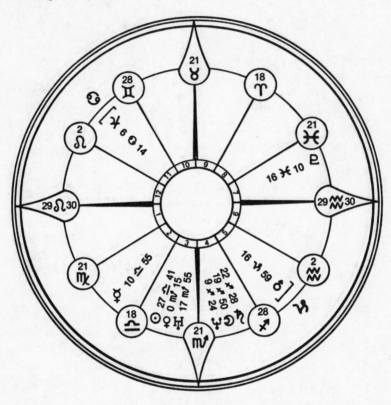

[Source: M.E. Jones]

Napoleon Bonaparte
August 15, 1769; 9:51 AM
Ajaccio, Corsica

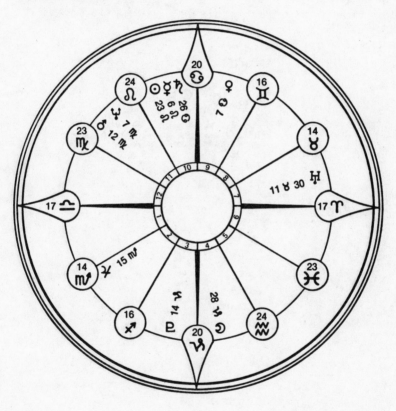

[Source: Grant Lewi]

Nicholas II, emperor of Russia
May 18, 1868; 12:02 PM
St. Petersburg (Leningrad), Russia

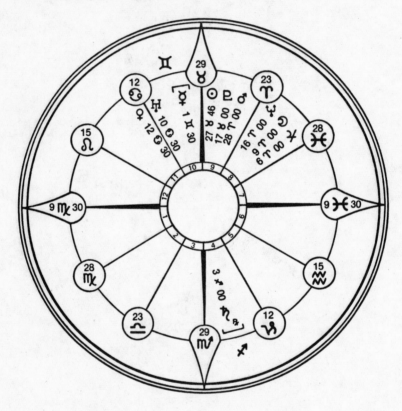

[Source: M.E. Jones]